Holy Ground

**THE RESOURCE ROOM
CHURCH HOUSE
9 THE CLOSE
WINCHESTER
SO23 9LS**

Holy Ground

"Put off thy shoes from thy feet, for the place whereon thou standest is holy ground."

Exodus 3:5

George Target

Bishopsgate Press Ltd
37 Union Street, London SE1 1SE

© 1986 George Target

British Library Cataloguing in Publication Data

Target, George
  Holy Ground.
  1. Shrines — Great Britain
  2. Great Britain — Description and travel — 1971 —
  I Title
  914.1' 04858   DA632

  ISBN 0 900 873 82 5
       0 900 873 83 3 Pbk

All enquiries and requests relevant to this title should be sent to the publisher, Bishopsgate Press Ltd., 37 Union Street, London SE1 1SE.

Printed in Great Britain by
Whitstable Litho Ltd., Whitstable, Kent

Contents

Introduction

It must remain a mystery why some places seem holier than others: the happy acceptance of the fact is the source of this book.

First, that word *holy*.

A rich descent to us from the Anglo-Saxon *halig*, describing all things which must be kept inviolate, complete, or whole, in unity. So, when the early English accepted Christianity, the word was already polished by use to translate the Latin ideas of *sacer* and *sanctus*, from which we derive *sacred, sanctuary*, and *saint*.

And *halig* soon became *hale* or *healthy*, and other words flowered: *hallow, hallowed . . . whole, holy . . .* all containing the meaning that to be *holy* is to be *whole*, and that to be *whole* is to be *healthy . . . complete* and *at one* with all that is.

Which implies that any consideration of true holiness, as opposed to ecclesiastical piety, can't simply be "about" your standard enshrined saints (some of whom we should properly regard as mad or deranged or sexually perverted), but must also include all manner of other much healthier holiness . . . beauty, truth, the presence of the Divine no matter where it is to be found, the experience and worship of those who celebrated wholeness and healing, who loved and enjoyed, and gave delight and pleasure and brought peace.

★ ★ ★

And there are two good ways to be seeing *these* holy places: with the eyes of a child or the faith of a pilgrim.

Visit any of them as a sceptic, and you'll only see what you know – the loss being your own, surely.

Join the crowds of tourists, and you'll pay through the purse at the clanking turnstiles, and end your day with aching feet and a fine clutch of tatty souvenirs.

How can I be so dogmatic?

Well now, wait while I tell you about St Patrick, the greatest stage Irishmen of them all, as I was told myself as a boy in the

Holy Land of Ireland . . . for there's a truth in the telling you won't be finding in the dreary facts, not if you searched from this mortal day to the green door of your own deep grave.

And Himself not even Irish.

*   *   *

Patrick, then, a sinner, the least learned of men, least of all the faithful – and didn't he confess so himself? And who are the likes of us to be arguing?

Though he came of decent people, Cumbria or Somerset or wherever, born of a natural woman in Roman Britain one year of the long ago, with no scholar among you knowing for sure which it was, give or take ten years or twelve of the fourth century or fifth.

But at fifteen or sixteen wasn't he seized by Irish raiders, so he was, and held captive in the Wood of Lochlut, "the oldest wood that ever was in Ireland" says he, "and the gloomiest". Yet there he "made friends with the wee children", and learned the Gaelic, and "the ways of the Irish". . . and wouldn't *that* be hard enough for any man? saint or sinner? Then he was taken to Country Antrim, sold as a slave to a chieftain, and held the six years or seven of servitude as a shepherd beyond the back hills of that land, always out in the rain falling, running this way and that after the mountain ewes and their lambs, and it a Pagan and distressful country, surely, unholy with fire and shed blood and other madness.

Though even as the longest hours of dark have a dawning, so his six years or seven had an ending, for one bold morning of June or July he was led by a voice to walk the length of that way from the back of those hills beyond, with never a dog to bark, nor man to stir or woman wake. Over rock and down glen was he led, through forest and marsh, this track and that green field, with many a stream and river to cross . . . until didn't he come to the wide shore, and the fine ship waiting, the sail unfurling.

And what embracings and kissings when he reached the door of home, and it open, what feasting and dancing and the telling of his tale, the hymns and the praises for the holy miracle of his deliverance! And what rest for the soles of his two feet!

But always, always, at noon of day and in the dark of night, always he heard the pleading of the Pagan Irish, crying as with one voice: "We beg you, holy youth, come back and walk once more among us".

And he would remember the blood and the fire of that distressful country, the weasels and wild cats, the armies and red gold, the long battles and longer slaughterings, the bodies of the dead and the cries of the wounded, the weeping of the mothers and sisters and new widows, the crying of the children left fatherless, the chanting of the Druid priests circling the indifferent stones, the useless sacrifices, the waste, the sad waste.

So what would he do but go back, study in France for to be a holy priest of the One True and Living God, so he did, another six years or seven, learn the mysteries of the Gospel, all the prayers of power, all the hymns, all the praises . . . and go back to that wide shore in answer to the pleading of the Irish.

And what wanderings from his landing, what great wonders, what journeyings and miracles! Because from the grey of dawn to the dark of night he went from here to there and on to beyond elsewhere, on his two worn feet and welted knees, this day and tomorrow and the long days after . . . and always would be brought the blind and the deaf and the dumb and those without sense from their birth, and the halt and the lame and those suffering from the palsy, and he would heal them for all the world to see, so he would, saying the prayers of power, and him not fearing prince nor priest nor any fighting-man of them at all, nor the rough curses in their mouths.

Many were the places in Pagan Ireland where Patrick walked on his own two holy feet, so he did, with the knees of him welted from the kneeling at his devotions, and him praying East and West, preaching the fine words of the Gospel North and South, with never a moment to be sparing at all.

And 'twas Himself sure that set the shamrock to be explaining the Trinity to the unlearned . . . and didn't he climb up the Hill of Slane on the northern banks of the River Boyne to kindle the Paschal fire on that first Irish Easter Saturday to be shaming the fires of the Druid priests from that good day to this.

Then away over to Tara of the High Kings where, on the Easter Saturday, in the great hall of the castle, and it now but a sad ruin, he bearded King Leary himself, and preached about

9

the holy meaning of the fire he'd lit, and drank without harm the poisoned cup prepared to his death by those same priests, and them all cast down by the miracle.

And on westward to Mag Slecht, the place of prostration, high on a shelf of limestone above Loch Crew, where he had the destroying of the idols of Crom Cruach with one shout of his holy mouth, and it as loud as the sound of many waters, and them the altars of human sacrifice, so they were, there to this day, the very stones a curse.

With no time now for the telling of every deed he did, the which, if they should be told every one, even Ireland itself could not contain the tales that could be told.

But the one – and it as true as grows the grass of the field.

For didn't he walk the soles of his two holy feet, and his poor welted knees, and strike across the round of the changing world with his face set for the Mountain of Croagh, neither man nor woman in his company, only a great bell for to sound in his loneliness. And didn't he climb up in the Lent of the year, and pray on the highest reach there for forty days and forty nights, that being the proper length of such holy vigils, go day, come night, God send another deliverance. And didn't the bleak winds assail him, and these birds of darkness clamouring and croaking about his holy head to the deafening of him, nor food nor drink to be passing his holy lips, and him praying East and West, with the fine words North and South . . . until, go night, come day, he had the powers of Hell defeated and destroyed, with these birds of darkness flapping away to the four corners of nowhere.

And then he wrested a promise from the very Angels of God that Ireland would keep the Faith until the Second Coming of Christ in glory on the clouds of Heaven. Amen.

And then didn't he hurl his great bell from him in triumph down the wicked chasm of Lugnagel on the side of the Mountain of Croagh, and why wouldn't he? with it clanking and clattering to be waking the sleeping dead, and the Angels of God tossing it back for him to be hurling down again, the noise astounding, so it was, with all the demons of darkness, and even the very serpents, tails in their mouths, bowling along like hoops, fleeing from that place for the fearful disturbance he was making with his two holy hands . . . so that to this day you'll

10

never have the finding of serpent nor demon in Ireland. Many another wicked thing remains, to the shaming of the Irish, surely, North and South, East and West, but never a natural snake nor strutting demon.

And isn't that same bell now to be found in its last true resting place, a niche in the Treasure House of Dublin, the Seventh City of Christendom, and it in a precious shrine made at the expense of Donal MacLoughlin, High King of Ireland, one year of the long ago.

★ ★ ★

And that's the story, or short part of it, which used to be told around the hearth-fires of Ireland . . . with, so I'm now instructed, never the word of factual truth in it at all.

"How much genuine tradition in regard to persons and places these legends may contain", it says here, "is largely a matter of speculation".

And who'll be arguing with the likes of your grand scholars?

Except that anything so powerful as such a legend must at least be a ripple on the surface of deep waters. The Irish lived in a comparatively stable society, had a rich and complex culture, a long Bardic tradition in which the Poet was honoured, their decorative crafts were unrivalled, and their religion was an integral part of their days and seasons . . . and yet it was all overthrown, changed, utterly changed by the coming of Christianity. Something tremendous happened in and to Ireland – and, in its own strange way, the legend of Patrick matches the dynamic of historical events. And why wouldn't it?

Because legends and myths are a poetic form of narrative shorthand, not always well served by translation into the one-dimensional language of prose sense – and symbols are better understood at a deeper level than scholarly reason, being the visible form through which is suggested the spiritual reality moving upon the face of the unfathomed waters of the soul. For example, we struggle to express our love in words . . . when a gentle kiss or touch of the hand will say more than any words – and one tear can tell the sorrow of the world. These are signs and symbols which have always been understood, for there are no adequate words to translate the language of the soul . . . with

11

myths and legends being the dialects of that language.

"As above, so below", say the mystics . . . meaning that the health of the individual soul is a mirror of the social order: if the spirit withers, so will the world in which we live.

"Fact is not the truth of myth", says Kathleen Raine, herself a Poet, "myth is the truth of fact".

But haven't those slithering snakes the worrying of some!

"A certain misconception is current", says one scholar, "as to the nature of the so-called lack of serpents in Ireland. St Patrick reputedly banished the creatures . . . and consequently they are supposed not to figure in the mythology. This is by no means correct".

True, as the serpent is "perhaps the most impressive and most truly typical of the Celtic cult animals". And aren't there snakes enough to be sparing in song and story?

"So", says your scholar, "any lack of serpent lore in Ireland is due to the deliberate suppression of all references to this sacred Pagan animal by the Church".

That, apparently, being the "meaning" of the legend: the story of St Patrick merely "tells" what the Church in fact did. And you can't be saying much fairer than that, surely?

Though it's never the ending of "explanations" at all!

Because yet other scholars do say that it has to do with the ending of the Ice Age ten thousand years ago, the glaciers melting and the waters of the sea rising, so that Ireland was cut off from Britain as Britain was cut off from Europe, with poor wee creatures such as snakes and moles never getting the chance to spread there.

Though, to tell you my own truth, I'd as lief leave it on St Patrick's holy platter as believe *some* of the scientific tales we're told! Not that Himself could programme a computer, nor even have the understanding of a pocket-calculator . . . except that he was there when the morning stars sang together, knew the sweet influences of Pleiades, and dwelt and abided on the rock, upon the crag of the rock, and the strong place.

*   *   *

For didn't I climb the Mountain of Croagh Patrick myself as a boy, and it a great cone of quartz rearing two-thousand-five-hundred-and-ten feet from the plain on the southern side of Clew Bay on the Atlantic Coast of County Mayo, so it is, and that a hard path and a tall climb for any full-grown man or natural woman, surely, let alone the legs of a child.

With that day as clear to me now as it was then, for all your scholars.

The gentle approach over the flat fields, the track up and through the heather of the front slopes, then the first winding steep ascent, the sharp stones and heaving boulders, the narrow ridge with a grand view of the purple mountains of Connemar away across the valleys to the south, and then the breathless ascent of that cone of quartz above and beyond, hands and knees and every finger, clambering round rather than directly up, view after view, distance upon distance, vistas of blue rememberings . . . until there was the Atlantic shimmering like a shield of hammered bronze, and *there* the final summit. Amen.

And what sights to be seen from there: the mountains to the south, the broad lands to the east, the scattered islands of Clew Bay below, and the mountain of Nephin Beg to the north beyond, and the great dreaming island of Clare out to the west in the waves of the Atlantic, and them heaving and surging from across the slow curve of the world.

With all that a glimpse into *another* world, where Time was Eternity, and a Perpetual Sabbath, the place standing in the centre of our lost Eden . . . a gift otherwise unattainable than by *being* there as a child of innocence or a beginner in wisdom.

For the skies and the earth and the air were Heavenly joys, that sea flowed in my veins, I was clothed with the summer sun and crowned with the unseen stars, the sole inheritor of the whole and holy universe, with every other child an inheritor, and every man and woman if so they chose, with none forbidden to enter into *this* Kingdom.

And to think that Thomas Traherne never set foot in Ireland.

But, do and say all, remain as sceptical as you have need, behind that apparent reality, beyond the mere rocks and islands, even above the summit and the scudding clouds, and certainly beneath the dark caverns of the mountain, within the depths of the experience, there was a truth on the far side of words . . . intimations of another order, whispers of immortality in that language of the soul, a music of silence.

And all you ever have to do is listen, become as a little child, walk as a pilgrim, tread on *any* holy ground. But mostly be still, stop dashing about . . . merely listen to what your heart will be telling you. Because the heart has its reasons . . .

★   ★   ★

Which, I agree, is easier written than believed, easier believed than done . . . because, driven by what we think are the imperatives of dates, deadlines, appointments, jobs that "have" to be finished by yesterday at latest, we become case-hardened against the enjoyment of the *now*, dulled to the rhythms of the living present.

"The Rule is", said the White Queen to Alice, "jam tomorrow and jam yesterday – but never jam today".

Yes, things were lovely when we were children, all those long warm afternoons of endless August by the seaside . . . and, if we cast our vote for the loudest political party, keep our shoulders to the wheel, productivity will improve by the end of the decade, unemployment will decrease, inflation come down, and we'll all get a larger slice of the national cake . . . tomorrow.

Behind us is the packaged past, instant nostalgia, the Golden Oldies, All Our Yesterdays . . . and the future arrives sooner, with more and more of it sounding terrible.

But what of our here and now? our continuous present?

Well, we obviously live at a time when Holy Days have become holidays, when the Sacred is now the secular in gaudy Technicolor, when "Heavenly" is a word to describe chocolate, "Hell on earth" is going to work in a crowded bus on a wet Monday morning . . . and where "God" is, er, "perhaps arguably the more or less existential ground of our, er, ultimate assumptions", or something.

The "weather" is merely what they attempt to predict at the Meteorological Office, no longer the slow cyclic changes in the seasons: what we are told about just before the News on television, and can see sometimes actually happening in that strip of sky between buildings . . . no longer the image of the whole earth in action. All we have to do is switch-on the central-heating and air-conditioning.

To survive in the olden days it was necessary to live in

harmony with what were accepted as the "Forces of Nature" . . . we had to invoke these unseen powers, or perish. Now we think we can control them – for are we not Masters of the Atom?

The experience of the passing year was once marked by Feasts and Celebrations and Rituals and Intercessions and Thanksgivings: Holy Times at Holy Places. Now there are Bank Holidays when Commerce gives itself a rest from computing all those billions . . . and we watch documentary television programmes about those quaint goings-on with that Obby Oss at Padstow, or would-be "Druids" traipsing around in white sheets at Stonehenge on, er . . . *what* day is it?

Winter is when we wear our thermal vests and pay higher fuel bills, on Shrove Tuesday we eat pancakes, at Easter it's chocolate eggs for the kiddies, May Day is now Labour Day and transferred to the first Monday of the month – chance for the Lefties to shout their heads off on a demmo. During Summer we take our annual fortnight on the Costa del Brochure . . . and at the beginning of November, after Guy Fawkes, we start getting ready for Christmas and all those expensive cards and presents and headaches.

What about Harvest Festival? Always put on a nice show, don't they?

Well, at least *that* used to be real: if there was a bad harvest there was nothing to feast about, little to eat, and less to waste on show. But, these days, to the sound of Musak, the supermarkets provide an endless harvest all the year long, our deep-freezers daily yield us their fruits of increase . . . and our churches are more likely to display a few packets of digestive biscuits than a real sheaf of wheat. Where would they get one, anyway? It's all cut by combines.

⋆   ⋆   ⋆

Yes, many of us are beginning to have doubts about the Brave New World of Science and Technology, and the Vision of a Golden Age offers us an alternative: the Way of Mystery rather than that of attempted Mastery . . . the greening of the landscape, not gridding it.

"Imagination is the real and eternal world", wrote William Blake, "of which this universe is but a shadow, in which we shall

15

live in our eternal or imaginative bodies when these mortal bodies are no more".

That's the open secret: imagination.

Lack of it is the curse of the contemporary world – we can't *see* what is happening to us today, and *refuse* to see what will happen to us tomorrow.

And to go to a holy place, walk on holy ground, to open yourself to its influence, is to have your imagination stirred, awakened, resurrected into fullness of life . . . to be taught how to feel, to experience, to *see* into that "real and eternal world". Because there's otherwise incommunicable knowledge to be gained through these moments of perception, eternity to be seen as the flash of fire on the wing of a kingfisher, immortal diamonds to be held in the palm of your hand, the hidden universe to be comprehended, the limitations of time and space to be wandered through as easily as passing from the shadow of trees into a shaft of sunlight.

"As above, so below . . ."

As in Heaven, so it could be on earth: as in us, so the universe.

All that is, the macrocosm, is reflected in all we are, the microcosm.

Within us we contain an inner cosmos: "Eternity opens from the centre of an atom".

And every holy place, every yard of holy ground, can be such a "still centre" from which to reach that great wheel of stars where the "fire and the rose are one".

*　　*　　*

We all know that sudden mysterious feeling . . .

A view of the full moon, huge as Jerusalem, high over the autumnal sea . . . or the bronze gong of the sun descending into the mists of a winter landscape.

The citidels of stars glistering at midnight . . . known, named, remote.

That dampness and chilling gloom of a cave, the promise and threat of almost touchable darkness . . . the silence you can almost hear . . .

The stillness in the depths of a forest . . . shadows, faint rustling . . . Distant spires and towers, crumbling walls, feet-

16

worn pavements, pillars, truncated arches, broken traceries . . .
"bare ruined choirs where late the sweet birds sang . . ."

Sunlight flickering through leaves, dappling, silvering the
dark green waters of a stream, the slow ripples now dazzling . . .

"Great stones on the upland, and green ways winding across
the chalk".

All of these may stir your imagination, reach the depths,
arouse the distant echoes of some ancient time when fear and joy
danced to the same drum . . . "the time of milking and the time
of harvest . . ."

"There is a feeling which comes to many sensitive people at
ancient sites", says John Michell, and him a writer of many
strangely mysterious books, "that they are standing on ground
which is in some way inherently sacred". He compares this
feeling with the "experience of dowsers or water-diviners", who
respond bodily to their awareness of underground water: awe in
the presence of mystery, the slight tension of strangeness, an
intimation of being both insignificant and yet of tremendous
importance in that "other" world of values behind apparent
reality . . . these are "tokens" of "spiritual" water.

T. S. Eliot puts it this way:
> "For wherever a saint has dwelt, wherever a martyr
>   has given his blood for the blood of Christ,
> There is holy ground, and the sanctity shall not
>   depart from it
> Though armies trample over it, though sightseers
>   come with guide books looking over it . . ."

And the fact is that we mostly have a wish or even a need for
magical or supernatural events or experiences which defy
rational explanation. For a trival example, it's obvious that Uri
Geller can only fool credulous scientists, and wouldn't last ten
minutes under the scrutiny of any competent stage-magician:
indeed, he refuses to "perform" for those best qualified to
judge . . . yet, somehow, we *want* all that childish key-bending
and "mind reading" to be true. We suspect that they *are* tricks,
but need to believe in "powers" which the High Priests of
Science can't measure or control.

And, in happy fact, there are *also* some truths which reason
cannot formulate, some images which exist despite our lack of
understanding . . . and who, apart from psychiatrists, would

17

presume to snare a dream in a web of words?

You don't have to be able to read a computer print-out to be moved by mysteries.

*　　*　　*

A place is holy, then, if its special features have moved people, impressed them by an obvious involvement with another world than this, a concern for different values . . . *this* is where the Divine has dwelt among us, full of love and wrath. And it acquires deeper holiness by being thought holy.

Most of us retain this ability to respond: we don't always work out why, but we meet new people and like them at once. . . or we enter a house and know that those who live in it are happy or miserable, loving or murderous.

I have visited Rudyard Kipling's house, *Bateman's*, near the village of Burwash in the beautiful countryside of East Sussex, and experienced loneliness, desolation, the sense of loss, time closing in . . . felt myself drowning in the mud of the Somme during the First World War . . . heard the bugles calling from sad shires . . .

And I have stood in John Ruskin's bedroom at *Brantwood*, looking out on Coniston Water in the Lake District, and wept with joy and gratitude for his witness to truth and justice and loveliness . . . been aware of glory, helpless incoherence, madness, and simple human goodness.

So, occasionally, we come across a landscape or a building, and feel the presence of something more important than ourselves, the "Other Than", not indifferent to our concerns, but beyond the reach of our small passions . . . *there* around us, answered by that of the Divine within us, strangely pleased, even rejoicing – but leaving the response entirely up to us. Worship or walk away . . . the freedom is always yours.

It's as though we can, by responding, cause the Divine to respond even more in delight: there's what Charles Williams called an "exchange of joy". We have been given the "final privilege of owing everything to ourselves" as well as to the sources of such pleasures.

Some of these places are elemental: the tops of certain hills or mountains, weathered rocks, lonely caves in the wilderness,

18

small lakes, deep waters, groves of trees, glades far in the woods.

Other places are holy because holy men and women have lived and prayed and died there, become brothers and sisters in a larger family . . . because builders have then tried to house this holiness in brick and stone, craftsmen have embellished, pilgrims come to celebrate. Almost any old church or ruined abbey can move you as a holy place where "prayer has been valid" . . . and you can be at one with the ancient dead in them, experience the merging of the temporal world and the timeless moments of eternity, have "thoughts too deep for tears . . ."

Even some cathedrals retain this capacity to draw such a response from us, still have the peace that "passeth understanding", the trembling stillness that isn't stagnation. They have been used to mark the serious events of life: birth, the flow of being, death, the great cycle and return of the seasons, the celebration of the mysteries. They have been places of worship, schools, centres of art, symbols of faith, repositories of history, burial-grounds for saints, memorials to the Church Triumphant . . . and these intangibles seem to permeate our awareness.

Most systems of religious belief usually have special sites at which ceremonies are performed. They may be simple, merely natural features of the landscape felt to be holy on their own account, perhaps made sacred by a visitation or even the continued presence of the Divine . . . and marked only by a standing stone or a grove of trees. Or they may be great temples or cathedrals, actual dwelling-places for the very Gods and Goddesses, with nothing too elaborate for their structure, nothing too magnificent for their decoration and furnishing.

"This is the House of God", claims the inscription in many Christian churches and chapels, with some going so far as to suggest that they're also the "Gates of Heaven".

Mind you, the authorities in charge of most cathedrals often seem to put everything they can between us and these feelings of higher awareness: charges for admission, cadging for upkeep, the racks and stacks of tawdry junk in the gift-shops, the clatter of cash-registers, tea and coffee and fizzy drinks, Conducted Tours of the Crypt . . . the voice of the Official Guide being especially loud in the Sanctuary . . .

But holiness is its own purifier, and, by picking your days and times, avoiding crowds and most Big Performances, it is still just about possible to have your deepest emotions expressed in stone, to see the Light of Heaven through stained-glass . . . to stand at the "still point of the turning world . . ."

★   ★   ★

When such a place is also associated with some good or great man or woman, the beginning of some wide-ranging movement, an event which has "altered the tide of history", then there are other powers present, other forces at work . . . which we must be careful not to mistake for holiness.

To walk through the Tower of London is to be depressed by the cruelty of kings and queens, the ambition or weakness of those willing to obey them, the courage of their victims . . . but I would never think of the place as holy.

To be pushed and shoved with the crowds around Westminster Abbey is to be reminded of Pomp and Circumstance, the "glories of our blood and State", the display and arrogance of temporal power, the ruthlessness of greed for riches or fame. Yes, the architecture is often magnificent behind all those florid monuments, the stained-glass is priceless, there are miracles of ecclesiastical craftsmanship . . . but are you on holy ground? Are these crowds pilgrims or tourists? Why is so much money changing hands? Is it a holy place or a commercial enterprise?

Yes, to look at St Paul's cathedral or York Minster, or the Chapel of King's College at Cambridge, is to be moved by all manner of grandeur, things of beautiful wood and carved stone, images of engraved gold and pierced silver and hammered bronze and sounding brass. Even the very words used to describe them are like fanfares on the high trumpets: Fan Vaulting, Rose Window, Clerestory, Tower, Spire, Pinnacle, Arch, Dome, Column, Crypt, Buttress, Transept . . . "everlastingly poetical and powerful", wrote John Ruskin. But neither the words nor the things are in themselves holy.

Agreed, beauty is a gift of the Divine, and to enjoy architecture and painting and sculpture and music and embroidery and liturgical language is to learn about the great mysteries of Creation and the Spirit . . . but sanctity doesn't depend upon them. And I have seen more holiness in the faces of young lovers than in all the cathedrals of this country, heard more of the harmony of Heaven in the laughter of a child than at umpteen Choral Evensongs . . . and watched Eternity unfolding in a wildflower.

Divinity needs no stage-management, for holiness begins in the heart, and then seeks a place in the world which will enable it to grow: the soul becomes aware of the "Other Than", and finds the holy ground where it may go on being happy.

To the true believer, child or pilgrim, all places are landscapes of the soul, everywhere is holy.

★   ★   ★

These landscapes are often obviously symbolic, already expression of truth deep within us . . . and the soul responds, like answers like.

For a well-known example, at the beginning of Dante's *Inferno* he finds himself in the Dark Wood, a "wild, rough, and stubborn" place, where the "straight way was lost" . . . which is the standard Medieval image for "Sin or Moral Ignorance", though not so much of "any specific act of sin", as that spiritual condition called "hardness of heart".

And mountains, as St Patrick knew fine, help some of us to test ourselves against a more demanding challenge, and climbing them is a natural image of the soul's ascent to the Divine. From their peaks we see a wider horizon, perhaps even a glimpse into the Promised Land, and the very summit represents the point of contact between Earth and Heaven, the intersection of the human and the Divine, time with Eternity. Though Gerard Manley Hopkins, in the terror of his despair, "pitched past pitch of grief", knew that the mountains of his mind had "cliffs of fall frightful, sheer, no-man-fathomed".

Yes, mountains remain mountains, but to know what they *can* represent is to be wise beyond the knowledge of geology.

Caves are penetrations into the earth, and thus into the body of the Great Mother, and have always been sacred and mysterious, even terrifying . . . and the Christian Virgin Mary still appears in grottoes.

Again, the still waters of a lake may be seen as an image of the serene soul reflecting the Divine as in a clouded mirror . . . or as the "waters of silence" running deep.

Rivers are equally obvious symbols of flow and continuity within continuous change, small beginnings leading to broad channels, the journey to the sea as an image of life returning to its source in Creation. Small islands and isolated rocks in that sea are natural places of solitude and concentration, enclosure by water as a means of purging the soul. And, of course, the sea is sustainer and destroyer, reminder of calm and storm, surface and depth, an image for the Voyage of Life, arrival and departure . . . with the ebb and flow of the dragging tides an ultimate acknowledgement of the Moon.

Yes, water is only water, but to understand such meanings is hardly the business of hydraulics.

And where there is water no night is wholly dark.

*　　*　　*

So we may thus bring our own feelings of awe into a place, project our own inner workings on to a blank screen, and worship images from our own depths . . . but, then, as the soul, so the world which the soul knows. Into the Dark Wood wander dark and tangled souls.

Another example, for various personal reasons the Contemplative monk or nun craves an austere life free from "worldy" distractions, and so retreats to the deserts to find a place solitary enough to meet those inner demands . . . and is often in danger of turning the Spiritual Life into a wilderness of negations. Whereas Thomas Traherne, the seventeenth-century English Mystic, remained an innocent all his life, saw his world of Civil War and religious persecution through the eyes of childhood . . . and "all things were spotless and pure and glorious" in the "peace of Eden", and he knew "those mysteries which the books of the learned never unfold".

All of which means that to visit a holy place is to give yourself the chance to be led across a landscape of dreams, perhaps by way of that Dark Wood . . . but out to the running rivers of collective remembrance, through "caverns measureless to man", and on "from swerve of shore to bend of bay", round and down to the "deep sea swell" where the great tides of human experience ebb and flow . . . to sink "full fathom five" where the bones of the dead "are of coral made", and "those are pearls that were their eyes . . ."

To walk on holy ground is to give yourself permission to experience the innocence of strong emotions, to ignore the false distinction between the Sacred and the allegedly "secular", to see the universal in the particular, the symbol in all things . . . myths as the contents of dreams. For even historians can merely try to record the facts which these myths have brought about.

Because myths and symbols are like the great fish of Jonah: they swallow us whole. We can never fathom their full meaning, no matter how deep that great fish dives. Such truths must always remain enigmatic, inexhaustible, irreducible. We live in a world where the pulpit stands higher than the altar, where the dead language of the Creeds is louder than Prophetic utterance . . . and we must restore the essential mysteries, or die in that final searing light of Technology, brighter than a thousand suns.

Yes, any First Year student of General Science at the University of East Anglia could probably demonstrate that Dante had got his cosmology all wrong . . . but I'll take the *Divine Comedy* on its own terms, where "Love moves the Sun and all the other Stars".

*   *   *

Dung to the earth, then, seed to the furrow, green shoot to the ripening sun, corn to the sickle, and from the corn the flour for our daily bread . . . even the Holy Bread.

Yes, it's all very old hat to the sophisticated: *The Golden Bough, From Ritual to Romance . . . The Waste Land . . .*

But unless we listen to our ancestral voices we're lost, for such simple truths are an essential depth of the mind, a dimension of necessary mystery to our limited understanding.

We need to deepen knowledge, not increase information.

Any competent teacher of mathematics can solve a simple algebraic equation: it takes a child at heart to convert the answer into apples we can eat . . . and our world is desperately short of such sweet golden apples of innocence.

Our planet is part of the whole universe, and we must once again become a whole and healthy part of our planet: we must love, not rape.

Because the new maps of Science are not the landscape, diagrams are not reality, the explanation is always less than the experience . . . and for too long we have "had the experience but missed the meaning". And without meaning we are "eye-deep in Hell".

It's no use looking back in anger, and even worse looking forward in fear: so why not try looking around in pleasure at the here and now?

★   ★   ★

There are holy places all over England, Ireland, Scotland, and Wales, and so I have ignored political divisions: who cares about politics except politicians?

And no ground needs to be blessed by bishops or moderators in order to be sanctified by the presence of the Divine, and so I have also ignored our "unhappy confusions", and described holy places in whatever acres of holy ground I've been able to reach behind the barbed-wire and turnstiles of dogma, prejudice, and commercialism: everywhere from Stonehenge to Walsingham by way of Cookham and Glastonbury . . . Roman Catholic, Anglican, Quaker, and happy Pagan.

With no loaded overtones of disapproval in the use of that word, as it simply derives from the Latin *pagus*, countryside – and where better place for wholeness and holiness?

Any standard guidebook will give you all the facts, all the proper names and precise dates, the bits and bobs of what passes for history . . . but you need to use your own eyes to see what's really going on, your own ears to listen to the music of the silence, your own willingness to understand the mysteries, your own imagination to enter into the spirit of the places.

I agree with Rowland Parker, whose book, *The Common Stream,* taught me the simple secret of sitting still on holy ground. "No book that I might write", he says, "could ever do as much for the sensitive mind as twenty minutes quiet contemplation in an ancient village church".

What *you* bring is as important as what's already there: even the holiest of ground can be marched over by great big clumping boots.

But please leave your camera at home: be aware of the holy

24

place in the fullness of your here and now, don't just peer one-eyed through the view-finder to "preserve" an image for afterwards. Live in the eternal present of the event, leave yourself open to all that's happening: sight, sound, touch, taste, smell. Otherwise all you'll have with a photograph or transparency is a one-dimensional illusion of reality . . . a fixed memory, not a living experience: a few coloured smears of synthetic chemicals on paper or plastic, not an interaction with the Divine which could change your whole life.

So take part, don't watch: belong to the celebration of holiness, don't be a tourist . . . be *in* your times and days to the full, don't pass through without touching the sides.

Because when you participate, when you become involved with what's going on, you have your feelings and imagination aroused, you experience bodily sensations, and grow warm to intuitions, aware of half-remembered dreams . . . other voices, another music than the one you know . . .

*   *   *

Yes, there *are* dangers in such free and easy wide openness.

"When people cease to believe in God", wrote G. K. Chesterton, "they won't believe in nothing – they will believe in everything".

And don't we just!

From Astrology to Zen, by way of Consciousness Raising, Dianetics, Freudian Psychiatry, Graphology, Parapsychology, Veganism, and you name it.

But to believe at all is enough for now, because life without belief is bread without a crust.

And theologians are demythologising Christianity, filleting out not only the pre-Christian bones but most of the Christian mystery as well, trying to build an Ecumenical wall against the future by undermining their own foundations.

There's a "more excellent way" . . . enriching rather than impoverishing, acknowledging the Myths rather than "explaining" them away, allowing that the essential mysteries must always remian mysterious.

"Better any number of Quests", says Geoffrey Ashe, himself a questing questioner, "even if some are illusory, than the arid pretence that there is no Quest at all".

So begin to understand your own worth, your significance in the "larger scheme of things" . . . hear the harmony, feel that inexplicable happiness, intense, even ecstatic.

Your past and future *are* eternally present . . . and your only time is in your here and now.

And the corn will be "orient and immortal wheat, which never should be reaped, nor was ever sown".

Come on, then, the holy places are waiting out there . . .

Though, with so much holy ground to be covering, there's no need to *loose thy shoes from off thy feet* . . . not unless you want to be walking bare-footed from now to the day of your mortal grave!

Earth Mother

Stonehenge ought to be the natural beginning of any warm-hearted pilgrimage to the holy ground of this country.

To start with, it's in the most magnificent landscape: the rolling Downs of Salisbury Plain, mile after windswept mile, an ocean of turf and pasture and heath, meandering valleys, streams, rivers, low hills, all you can see of the earth heaving and shouldering against the wide sky. These hills and ridges of chalk radiate over Southern England: the Downs, the Chilterns, Marlborough . . . with this Plain at the centre.

Chalk drains well, so the ancient peoples probably found it easier to travel along the ridgeways than through the marshes of the valleys . . . so it's understandable enough on our completely different terms why Stonehenge should have been built where their various routes met. Though they had other and more mysterious reasons, building and modifying and partly rebuilding for twelve hundred years . . . generation after generation, century after century . . .

And to stretch out on the far hills and look over the valley at those inscrutable arrangements of great stones is to be aware of these mysteries, to be in touch with the continuity of our country, to step back from the hourly news-bulletins and instant-replay history, and give yourself the chance to see that other world than this one which "is too much with us, late and soon, getting and spending . . ."

Be there very early in the morning before the crowds start to arrive, or stay long after they've gone in the evening. Watch the sun rise or set. Best of all, stay overnight in a tent, especially when the full moon arches through the Heaven-tree of stars.

True, you won't be permitted in at these magical times, barbed-wire will separate you from any close contact of the human kind, guard-dogs will snarl if you try to get in touch with your heritage. Unless, of course, you happen to be a member of a television crew making another documentary.

Because, as Wynford Vaughan-Thomas is not alone in pointing out, the place has "lost the original glory of its setting in the wide bareness of Salisbury Plain".

27

Yes, if it wasn't for that barbed-wire it would be vandalised, chipped away in souvenirs, daubed with all our usual words and slogans and frustrations. If there wasn't an Official Path around at a safe distance from the inner circles our hundreds of thousands of visiting feet would do in ten years what centuries of weather haven't done. "The balance between enjoyment and preservation is particularly delicate", say the Voices of the High Guardians. "Stonehenge has been given into the safe-keeping of the National Trust, and the Trust would be failing in its duty if it did not protect it from the threat of damage". And who could argue with that?

But the "protection" is also destroying it just as surely as the new barbarians ever would . . . except more subtly, and certainly not by any intention. Because to treat the past as a museum is to deny its power: yesterday is only of value if we allow it to breathe in the today of our continuous present.

To "preserve" is an attempt to arrest a natural process: birth, life, death, corruption putting on incorruption by nourishing that "immortal wheat" which has "stood from everlasting to everlasting".

"Dust to dust" is the essential principle of existence, "old timber to new fires" a necessity for the baking of bread . . . and then, inevitably, "old fire to ashes, and ashes to the earth . . ."

We live in a cycle of change: the possibility of permanence is a delusion.

"That which thou sowest is not quickened, except it die".

And not even Her Majesty's Department of the Environment can interfere with such a principle, and neither the National Trust nor English Heritage (which owns the site) can alter the "time of the seasons and the constellations . . ."

So, fortunately, Stonehenge abides . . . and you don't have to be able to get close enough to touch any of its stones to understand the power of them and to experience their mystery.

Anyway, from too close they're strangely disappointing, a bit drab, so much smaller and less dramatic than those photographs in the Sunday Colour Supplements . . . picturesque ruins, a meaningless jumble of boulders . . . doorways without doors . . .

"Not like it was on television", says the woman in the red dress. "Makes you wonder what all the fuss is about".

★   ★   ★

Don't, then, go too near that barbed-wire surrounding the area, avoid the Druid Motel and the cars and coaches crawling along the main roads, stay away from the tourists and trannies and clicking cameras and ice cream vans and stewed tea on sale in polystyrene-cups, ignore the long queue at the turnstile, keep your admission money in your pocket or purse, let others shuffle in flocks around the Official Path, and live without the latest "explanations" of when and how and why this "Ancient Monument" was built, forget the approved guidebooks and glossy postcards in the gift-shop . . .

And make your own way, have eyes to see, ears to hear, let your own two feet do the walking, understand with your imagination rather than your mind, go with the flow of the landscape, follow the curves of the Downs, find a place on the springing turf of those far hills, perhaps by one of the hundreds of burial-mounds clustered around the area, "vestiges of ancient times", stretch out, feel the earth beneath and the sky above, breathe in that fresh air, enjoy the free sunshine, smell the grass and the wildflowers, listen to the larks ascending, all those "profuse strains of unpremeditated art" . . . and then look over the valley . . . dream back to "flints and bronze and iron beginnings . . ."

Been there forty centuries, those stones . . . and the world they inhabit has not yet been created in our imaginations.

They're in no tearing hurry, so have your picnic, eat wholemeal bread and honest non-processed cheese, munch apples, drink fresh milk or real beer . . .

Four thousand years and more, seedtime and harvest, Summer and Winter, and day and night: birth, life, death . . .

If we don't destroy ourselves and the world, either slowly or suddenly, if we go in our own good time, full of years and vain regrets, night will still follow day across these hills, the cold Winter will always ease into the promise of Spring, dull roots will stir with warm rain, the corn will die that the corn can live . . .

So be at one with those who marked out the place and pattern of those circles, eat your bread-and-cheese and quarry those great stones, drink your beer and drag them all the miles from the distant mountains, feel your muscles aching, dig the pits down into the chalk, man-handle those enormous blocks, heave and push and lever them into position, one after another, hour after day after week after month after year over the four or five centuries of such work it needed for the building.

Is there anything *you'd* like to do which would demand such effort and resources during so long a time? What would move *us* to any comparable labour? The Channel Tunnel?

Why did those ancient peoples do it?

All we can do is speculate, and there are hundreds of books about the "problem" of Stonehenge, thousands of articles and broadcast talks and features and highly-coloured programmes on television: facts, theories, fancies . . .

"Exactly", says the Emeritus Professor of Archeology. "Indisputable facts about culture and religion depend almost entirely upon written records, and there *aren't* any such records from the period in question. Mere speculations simply encourages the lunatic fringe. Next question"?

*   *   *

The people who planned and built those circles of stone, and hundreds of other such circles all over Europe and this country, some smaller, many larger, lived four or five thousand years ago. They had been hunters and nomads, and were now farmers, growing wheat and barley, rearing cattle and sheep, occasionally hunting for fresh meat, fishing when they could. Their only tools were flints and stones, antlers and fire-sharpened sticks – and so their times have been called the New Stone Age.

Which, incidentally, reveals our technological bias: we see ourselves as the Great Technocrats, the manipulators of things, masters and entitled exploiters of the world and its resources, with Outer Space and the rest of the Universe now open before us . . . and we label our ancestors merely by the material of the tools they used. The *Old Stone Age* because their clubs and pounders were natural shapes that fitted the hand, the *New Stone Age* because axe-heads and scrapers and knives were now flaked and worked into more efficient cutting-edges, the *Bronze Age* because they had discovered how to use metal, the *Age of Iron* because they could build charcoal furnaces hot enough to smelt ore . . .

A more truly human description of those ancient times would be the *Age of the Great Mother* . . . even the *Golden Age* . . .

For one factor, not often remembered when we imagine them as heavily fur-clad against *our* sort of cold and damp weather, is that they had an excellent climate. "Warm temperate conditions that favoured their crops", writes William Anderson, and "cloudless night skies that enabled reliable and constant observation of the heavens".

Again, as far as can be certain from the scattered remains of a people with none of those "written records", it seems that their social and religious consciousness began with womanly concerns: menstruation, the connexion between copulation and pregnancy, birth.

This awareness was magical rather than intellectual, and had more to do with rituals than words: they identified with what they knew long before they ever shaped their "explanations" into coherent myths. They saw as children, making no distinction between themselves and the rest of their world: earth, air, fire, water, rocks, trees, birds, plants, animals, sun, moon, stars, men, women . . . everything existed in the here and now of the endless flow of being and becoming. And so they valued the natural cycle of life and death, growth and decay, continuity . . . instinct rather than self-will, functions rather than abstractions.

As above, so below: as inside, so outside: as the soul, so the world. All was one . . .

And holiness, or wholeness, oneness, though occasionally more manifest at ritual times in special places, was in everything . . . for the whole Earth was seen as the Great Mother, not merely everywhere-present but bone of Her bone, flesh of Her flesh, breath of Her breath: *She* was what there was, and *they* were part of Her processes.

31

Her names were many, but Her functions and attributes were simple and elemental: Her womb conceived and brought to birth all things necessary for life . . . and not merely food and water and clothing and fire, because she also granted knowledge of the seasons, the journeying of the Sun from the heights of Summer to the depths of the Winter Solstice, the waxing and waning of Herself as the Moon. She rode upon the storm, at Her will the warm winds were directed and tides ordained, Her footsteps were in the sea, and for Her the stars moved in their courses. On Her tongue were the languages of the trees and the naming of the months, health and healing were in Her hands, nurture and nourishment in Her breasts . . . and for Her the White Roebuck waited in the thicket, the Salmon leaped the hidden stream, and the Wild Red Boar came trotting at Her voice.

"From Her all proceeded, and to Her all returned", for She was also Mistress of the Dark Side of Her Moon, Lady of the lamentable silences of Death, Disposer of the Dead.

And there was harmony between the whole family of living things, a balanced giving and taking, a sense of unity . . . the dream of that Golden Age which has since haunted the collective memory of humanity: that time when Nature was Sacred, bountiful and yet dark with terror. *Those* people were at one with their awe-inspiring world: *we* occasionally drive out on a fine Sunday afternoon to a picnic in a Conservation Area.

*   *   *

Yes, agreed, that's idealised, sentimentally romantic – a Technicolored description of a society which has never yet existed in quite those happy matriarchal terms. And, to tell you the truth, when I remember *some* militant Feminists of our own day, I don't believe that *they* even want to bring it about, being more intent on destroying the present patriarchy.

But these are the countries of the mind, landscapes of the imagination, dreams rather than construction plans . . . yearnings, not claims to historical accuracy.

Though it's obvious that our fragmented society doesn't share this unified vision . . . but given a sympathetic imagination it's easy enough to understand how it might have worked.

In the domestic world of such a dream the hearth tended by women was the social focus of the family and the tribe, a source of warmth and comfort and food, light against the darkness, a sacred place. "Home", say the Irish to this day, "is where you make your fire, though it be with the tinkers in a ditch under the wheeling stars". And the great white mounds of their burial-chambers were at once a symbol of the tightly-packed heaps of ash in which women maintained the glowing charcoals, and also the pregnant belly into which the dead would be carried through a vaginal opening and passage back into the central womb . . . for women to bring forth fire and light from ashes by their breath, and also offer the promise of life from death, the prospect of resurrection from the tomb.

And then, after a wilderness of hunting and nomadic wanderings, as an extension of their daily food-gathering, nuts, berries, fruits, the first skills of farming were developed by women – who saw in the fruitfulness of the soil their own sexuality: the earth as womb, the seed as fertilising sperm, months of waiting, the resulting crops as both birth and harvest . . . the plough-stick as phallus, the hole or furrow as vagina, the coming together of earth and seed as copulation.

"The sexual union with the soil that is a constant feature of agricultural fertility rituals", writes Erich Neumann, "is based on the identity of the woman with earth and furrow, of the man with the plough. The naked recumbent Goddess is the Earth itself".

Again, women were in charge of the harvest, the grinding of the corn, the baking of bread, the saving of the seed for the next planting . . . for which they would weave the last sheaf of their gathering into a Corn Doll, a representation of the Great Mother and natural symbol of the Spirit of the Corn being kept alive through the bleak reign of the King of Winter – to be brought out sprouting in the Spring of the year, and sown with the bulk of the saved seed.

The Queen of Summer and the King of Winter, then, their turning times at Mid-Summer and Mid-Winter: the Goddess ruling until the death of Her Consort, the King of the Corn . . . when He is cut down in the harvest, and so dies to reign in death that Her people can eat and live.

And so the great Myths emerge . . .

Spring began to be seen as the mating of the Great Mother with the young Corn God. Late Summer, the time of harvest, was then the time of His inevitable death, when most vegetation died with Him. The womb of the earth was now the tomb of life, the Great Mother was a widow mourning Her dead lover, and She searched the chambers and realms under the hills for Him, the Queen of the Northern Stars became the Harrower of Hell. And then, triumphantly, She found Him in the warmed and watered seed, now sprouting, and bore Him yet again as Her Son and Kingly Consort . . . for them to mate once more at the beginning of another cycle: birth, copulation, death . . . continuous resurrection . . .

"In fertility and generation", remarked Plato at the time when these Myths were being written down as literature, "the earth sets an example to woman".

The functions of women were thus reflected and enhanced in the attributes of the Great Mother, with exuberant sexuality Her major blessing and joyous motherhood one of Her most precious gifts.

There was, moreover, a mysterious relationship between women of flesh and the spiritual nature of the Goddess . . . and that was the obvious numerical connexion between the cycle of menstruation, the regular sign of womanly fertility, and the monthly cycles of the moon: both twenty-eight days.

Indeed, the word menstruation derives from *menses*, the Latin plural of *mensis*, a month . . . with month deriving through the Old English, *monath*, from *mona*, the moon.

So, even in the history of words there's already a deeper relationship than the merely numerical . . . and She was especially worshipped (or given worth) as the Moon, that High Queen of the Night, the White Goddess.

Yes, the rising and setting of the sun marked their days . . . but the apparently inconstant moon was the measure of their first calendar. Each of the four phases could be counted through the four weeks of seven days which constituted the cycle from the first crescent of the new month to the last pale silverings. Thirteen such lunar months constitute one year of the sun – give or take a spare day every so often.

And so women and the White Goddess ebbed and flowed together, waxed and waned, measured out times and seasons, were mysterious, moved to their own cycles, responded to their own inner rhythms. Humanity now has many mechanically inhuman ways of measuring the passage of time, most of them involving a minute accuracy beyond any sensible need of life: children with digital wrist-watches can "tell the time" within one-hundreth of a second, an interval too fast for their eyes to see, and races are now won or lost by the literal thickness of a finger-nail. But the ancient cycles of the moon and menstruation remain, reminding us of a time "older than the time of chronometers", a time of buds and leaves, flowers and fruits, and then the bare fields and trees.

True, any biological connexion between these cycles is denied by many male gynecologists, there being little "scientific" proof, and large numbers of men still ignore menstruation as a fact of social life, regard it as an "illness", taboo, dirty, even disgusting, the point of crude "jokes" or sexist jibes. Which, of course, is *their* problem.

Because the White Goddess represents a different order of knowledge than that of our present sexually disturbed and technological society. "Sexology" is now a subject of solemn study in university laboratries, where scientists attempt to isolate and observe and measure with clinical precision what should be the indescribable ecstasies of whole and holy abandonment. Open-crotch nudies are the staple of porno-graphic magazines and video nasties. Popular newspapers print their daily flaunting of tits and bums. The fantasy of the "available" girl is the soft-focus image by which we are sold almost every consumer product from cigarettes to lavatory-paper. And the Instant Moralists swallow and sweat even at the innocence of truly human nakedness.

We are thus desperately restricted within the arbitrary limits of what we can actually measure: we reduce the universe to a place of rules and dials and scales and diagrams, "explanations" and "sufficient reasons" and impoverishment.

Whereas She was One with Her people, they danced to a different drum, lived by rhythms we mostly can no longer experience, knew powers we can't even begin to programme on any computer.

And Her people saw their lives and their myths *as* one, a unity of belief and action. The myths didn't "explain" the mystery,

35

but *were* mysterious: their religion *was* their technology. What they *believed,* they *did.* The earth provided food for the soul as well as the body.

This Divine Matriarchy was thus supported by a deeply satisfying Myth which governed the forms of society, and was revealed as true by every process in the various cycles of their year: the waxing and waning of the moon and women, the coming and going of the sun and the seasons . . . birth and death, decay and resurrection. And it was a life where story, song, poetry, dance, drama, crafts, architecture, and art were all necessary for successful hunting, the growing and harvesting of crops, the breeding of cattle, the birthing of children, and the comfort and safety of the dead . . . and where everybody shared in the communal life and pleasures of the tribe. All things were Sacred, and so life was sacramental . . . the secular hadn't yet been invented.

And the White Goddess was worshipped as the Supreme Deity, Queen of Heaven and Earth, from the beginning of the New Stone Age, around seven thousand years before Christ, until the desecration and destruction of Her temples by the early Christian Church. Moreover, on the evidence of many happily sexual or hugely pregnant figurines and statues, some archeologists would extend Her supremacy as far back into pre-history as twenty-five thousand years before the Hebrew-Christian God Jehovah first spoke to Abraham.

"These figures of the Great Mother", writes Erich Neumann, "are representations of the Goddess of pregnancy and child-bearing . . . the archetypal symbol of fertility, and of the sheltering, protecting, and nourishing elementary character".

Yes, the priests and theologians of our male-dominated Jewish and Christian religions have taught that these ages were Pagan and idolatrous, dark and chaotic, wicked and sinful, lacking all claims to sanctity . . . though some Christians still refer wistfully to their "Mother Church", as though to make up for the lack of feminine influence. Yet as a contemporary Feminist scholar, Merlin Stone, points out, "it has been archelogically confirmed that the earliest law, government, medicine, agriculture, architecture, metallurgy, wheeled vehicles, ceramics, textiles, and written language were initially developed in societies that worshipped the Goddess".

36

True, we have carried those developments to extremes of technology which would have terrified our ancestors – and terrify some of us: weapons of nuclear, biological, and chemical warfare by comparison with which their clubs of stone are merciful . . . an agribusiness that is rapidly reducing the earth to a wilderness . . . a Space Industry which regards the moon as merely a possible satellite for use in our coming Star Wars.

With us the church is at the other end of the High Street from the supermarket: one "offers" Spiritual Bread . . . the other provides a pre-sliced, vitamin-enriched, chemically-flavoured, starch-reduced substitute for real bread. And even "our" God is now a subject for intellectual debate among bishops and clergy at Yearly Synod.

*　　*　　*

Everything those ancient peoples saw or heard or experienced was symbolic, and this symbolism fed-back into and inspired the very way they saw or heard or experienced . .˙. from the growing of the grass to the movements of the stars in their courses.

To demand a detailed explanation of what, precisely, these symbols were symbolising is to miss their significance, limit their meaning, set another futile question in a theological examination paper. The point is to experience the mystery, not reduce it to one-dimensional prose: not to "explain" but to accept.

For example, they saw the whole of their landscape as the living body of their Great Mother: what to us are the far hills, mere valleys and woods and streams, were to them Her flesh. She not only sprawled across the earth, but *was* the earth, there in every curve and fold and secret place . . . with even the very chalk *Her* sacred colour, *Her* mark by which She was to be known. That was Her broad back along the distant horizon, those mountains and rocks Her bones, these lovely swellings Her breasts, all archings Her great thighs, all thickets Her hair, and Her pregnant belly heaved beneath them. Her veins were the rivers, Her blood flowed in the sap, Her milk bubbled from the springs, Her sweet juices ran in abundance everywhere. And her breathings were the winds, Her sleepings the night,

Her dreams their visions, Her awakenings the dawning of each new day.

"The earth was seen as a living body", write Janet and Colin Bord, "from which came life, and to which all life returned".

However strange this may sound to the literal mind, it's a familiar concept to the poetic imagination . . . and isn't the Moon the Muse of True Poets?

William Blake, for one, had the Vision of Albion, who "anciently contain'd in His mighty limbs all things in Heaven and Earth", and was "fettered" within the hills and valleys of our land, His form obscured by the encroaching fogs of grey misery, His Spiritual Kingdom "usurped" and "ravaged" by the "dark Satanic mills" of "false Philosophy", wrong-headed Science, profit-motivated Industrialists, and petty-minded Politicians.

And who of us, with this morning's newspapers in hand, would deny the truth of this prophetic nightmare?

But these ancient peoples did more than merely see with an intense clarity what they believed was already there.

Yes, the Great Mother was already present . . . and Her believers depended on Her for their crops, animals, and daily life. All was one, and so they made their world an extension of themselves by reshaping and emphasising the evocative forms of the downland. They moulded the very earth of Her flesh in homage, moved hills, dug enormous dykes and ditches in sacred patterns, engineered gigantic mounds and long barrows and tremendous walls of chalk around especially holy places, built stone rings of various shapes and sizes, circles, ellipses, straight or curved avenues . . . all to manifest Her presence more generously, to make Her even more evident, to add further significance to what they saw.

Does the land wait for the sleeping Mother to wake? Or is the lovely land that very Mother who sleeps?

The whole and holy world was their sculpture.

Sometimes they incised huge outlines of Her and Her various fertilising Consorts on the sides of the hills.

One of the most interesting of these representations is cut in the slope below Wandlebury Camp along the Gogmagog Hills near Cambridge. There's an enormous woman with a great round moon-face and staring eyes, a horse on which she's riding, a chariot, and the crescent of the waning moon above. To the right there's a warrior with a shield, his sword raised over his head, and to the left there's another man with the rays of the sun emerging from his forehead. T. C. Lethbridge, the brilliantly unorthodox archelogist who discovered them beneath the overgrown turf, identified them as the Moon Goddess and Earth Mother, with Her Consort the Sun God, and Wandil, a local God after whom Wandlebury is named. True, the orthodox dismiss it all as a nineteenth-century fake, rather in the spirit of Piltdown Man . . . but they offer no evidence of any such work being done – and how could the digging of such gigantic figures have been missed?

Again, on the side of the hill north of Cerne Abbas, close to the immense earth ramparts of Maiden Castle, a Stone Age city near Dorchester in Dorset, there's an even larger naked man outlined in the turf. He brandishes a great club in his right hand, has a disproportionately engorged erection, and is the only survivor of a similar group of figures. Women used to sit or lie between the testicles, or have sexual intercourse there, as a cure for barrenness.

The largest of all such figures is on Windover Hill, near Wilmington, Sussex, two-hundred-and-thirty feet tall. He stand straddled and upright, his arms spread wide, with a staff as long as he is in each hand . . . but emasculated, probably by early Christians.

Many people believe that there must be dozens of these tremendous figures lost beneath the grass all over the country . . . and perhaps William Blake may have seen some of them.

However, these ancient peoples did more than incise the hills: they built artificial hills and earth-works of their own, with many earth-circles obviously womb-like in shape . . . shifted millions of tons of soil and chalk, quarried and transported thousands of great stones, laboured for hundreds of years . . . all as a continuous act of what often seems obsessive worship.

Which many of us find hard to understand. When *we* see earth-works on the tops of hills we almost automatically think of fortifications, fighting, attacks and defence, war and violence – and can't imagine why any people should build such places unless for *our* reasons.

For instance, quite close to Stonehenge there's Figsbury Ring, a lovely circular ditch and earth-wall enclosing an expanse of lush grass, with magnificent views of the surrounding countryside . . . including Porton Down. Well, in Porton Down there are scientists, some of the most brilliant people in the world, at daily work on weapons of chemical and biological warfare, researching the means of killing hundreds of millions of our Brothers and Sisters in ways too terrible to bear much thinking about. And all along the beautiful track up to the Ring, partly hidden by tall grasses and creeping wildflowers, there are these brutal warnings: DANGER KEEP OUT . . . barbed-wire, secret surveillance, the presence of most horrible death . . .

And Figsbury Ring is described as a "fort" . . .

Well, yes, we would, wouldn't we?

They lived and built up on the hills and along the ridges because these were the holy places and centres of power . . . *we* reserve our greatest national efforts for war: we unite only to kill . . .our major engineering works are devoted to motor-ways and tunnels and bridges to get us from here to there and back again just those few minutes quicker . . . nuclear power-stations produce energy we don't need, dangerously, with wastes which will contaminate the oceans for tens of thousands of years . . . and we reach for the stars to better destroy those we are told are our enemies on earth.

And yet some of us dare to call our Stone Age ancestors savages.

"Not long out of the caves, were they?"

But it's an impoverishment to judge them and their ideas by our own twentieth-century standards: civilisation isn't technology. Yes, we can fly from London to New York in three hours . . . but is either place "civilised" in any fully human sense?

★ ★ ★

Savages or not, they had a practical knowledge of astronomy, geometry, mathematics, and land-surveying that was only equalled by the early Greeks a thousand or more years later.

The sites of their works of worship are arranged in various

systems across the whole landscape, occuring at regular distances, and aligned with each other in mysterious straight lines . . . from the centre of a stone circle here to one standing stone on the far horizon, then to a cairn beyond the next valley, on to a dolmen, an artificial bank, another circle, an earth-mound, then a length of track-way, or along a stream, on and on . . . even to the Region of the Summer Stars.

There are hundreds of these alignments, some comparatively short, some extending for miles and miles. One of the longest, for example, starts at St Michael's Mount, near Marazion in Cornwall, a legendary and holy place in its own right, which used to be part of the lost Land of Lyonesse. A straight line from there passes through the Cheesewring on Bodmin Moor, a weird tower of huge rocks, claimed by sceptics to be the result of "natural formation and weathering", but believed by the imaginative to be the "remains of vast interconnected power-storage temples". The line then passes through St Michael's church on Brentor in the wastes of Dartmoor – it being more than merely interesting that so many churches built on hilltops or pre-Christian mounds are dedicated to St Michael. Then on to Burrow Mump at Burrow Bridge in Somerset, a large prehistoric burial mound with another church dedicated to him on top. Then Glastonbury, then Avebury Ring south of Stonehenge, and so on and on eastwards, more or less following the track of the Icknield Way, through Bury St Edmunds, on to the coast of the North Sea near Lowestoft . . . with many other old churches and earthworks and standing stones all along the line.

True, you can dismiss it as a series of coincidences . . . but you'd be straining at facts.

⋆　　⋆　　⋆

These alignments, of course, are the famous (or notorious) "ley-lines" . . . about which academic controversy continues to bicker and trickle.

The idea is based on the acceptance of an imaginative truth: that there is indeed a mystery concealed within the landscape, patterns, deliberate arrangements . . . "whereby", says John Michell, "every one of the innumerable structures of antiquity

41

was sited and shaped in accordance with principles quite unrecognised by modern science". He calls this "terrestrial geometry", and its facts are hardly to be disputed . . . merely their interpretation.

True, the orthodox hold that the claim "exceeds the limited evidence", and "in any case is surely a distinct improbability".

These "principles" were rediscovered at the beginning of this century by Alfred Watkins, a magistrate, photographer, and enthusiastic antiquarian with a wide and deep knowledge of the countryside. On one of his many journeys he stopped on a high hill-top, "meditating on the view below him". And, suddenly, in a "moment of perception", he "saw" a web of straight lines spread across the country, "linking the holy places and sites of antiquity . . . exact alignments" that crossed "beacon hills to cairns and mountain peaks" by way of "mounds, old stones, crosses and old crossroads, churches placed on pre-Christian sites, legendary trees, moats and holy wells . . ."

Alfred Watkins called these lines "leys", adapting on old English word *lea*, originally meaning an "enclosed field", but which he suggested simply meant a grassy track . . . and he accepted them as roads or trade routes, with no mysterious overtones.

To the orthodox it all remains a puzzle, because the very idea that prehistoric peoples could measure and mark out the whole country in this precise and complete way contradicts all their assumptions . . . and those who believe that *their* assumptions are the only correct ones can never be convinced. Leys *must* be the invention of cranks and crackpots. End of discussion.

To the imaginative it's all a revelation, because though some of these alignments are obviously astronomical, and some are geographical, there are many others, equally "there" to all but the desperately orthodox, which are neither.

"There may be other forces", says John Michell, "once known in the remote past, whose exact nature has since been forgotten".

They have been called "meridians of cosmic energy", or "lines of flow for geo-physical power".

"There was an extensive system of constructions designed to channel the cosmic and planetary energies", claim Janet and Colin Bord, "which, when invoked and directed by mental control, would have a beneficial influence upon all forms of life . . . It was the original intention of early peoples to ensure the correctly balanced flow of life-giving energies throughout the world . . ."

"An injection of solar energy into the Ley system would occur", writes Anthony Roberts, "when the sun rose over the alignments . . . and the geometrically straight lines rearranged the flow of terrestrial currents, imparting a pattern of fertility and harmony to the land . . ."

"A principle of nature exists", wrote Guy Underwood, a solicitor and Justice of the Peace as enthusiastic and know-ledgeable as Alfred Watkins, "which appears to be generated within the Earth, causes perpendicular wave motion, forms spiral patterns, has great penetrative power, affects the nerve cells of animals, and is controlled by mathematical laws . . . I call it the Earth Force". And he found that this "force" ran in various straight or looped lines across the country, with many of them intersecting at traditional holy places . . . with Stone-henge the centre of a "kind of whirlpool" involving an "enormous loop forming an almost complete circle" around it, a "double-loop encircling the Heel Stone", and "dozens of minor eddies".

Penny plain, tuppence Technicolored . . .

Make your own choice.

The fact is, whether you accept the Technicolor flows and cosmic loopings or not, Stonehenge is undoubtedly built at the intersection of four penny-plain ley-lines . . . to one of which, delightfully, Salisbury cathedral is a very late addition.

This is no very difficult problem, because the Christian Church often absorbed ancient holy places and Pagan Gods and

Goddesses, and even the main Mid-Winter Festival (now Christmas), into the new Faith . . . with the full approval of pragmatic theology. "I have come to the conclusion", wrote Pope Gregory in the seventh century, specifically to his missionaries in Britain, "that the temples of the idols should not on any account be destroyed . . . smash the idols, but the temples should be sprinkled with holy water, and altars set up in them in which relics of the saints are to be enclosed. For we ought to take advantage of well-built temples . . . and dedicate them to the service of the true God. In this way, I hope the people will . . . continue to frequent the places as formerly . . ."

We'll see later how these temples reasserted themselves in the very churches and cathedrals built to replace them.

Anyway, most old churches and cathedrals are on these pre-Christian holy sites, along with chapels, monasteries, abbeys, and priories. Religions arise, thrive, degenerate, and die . . . but holiness obviously persists in the world, and answers a need in the human spirit.

*   *   *

Stonehenge, then, out there on Salisbury Plain at the centre of a system of power about which we know so little that the merely dogmatic ought to have the grace to remain silent.

In the Anglo-Norman twelfth century it was called "pierres pendre" in French, and "stanhengus" in English. Wace, the Anglo-Norman Poet, named it the "Place of Hanging Stones", and Henry of Huntingdon said that this was because "the stones hang as it were in the air" . . . which, as we'll see, may be a Folk memory of something "rich and strange . . ." So even the name is imaginative enough for those who "on honey-dew hath fed, and drunk the milk of Paradise".

Ditches and banks, isolated standing stones, a double-circle of seven-tonners from the Prescelly Mountains of South Wales over one-hundred-and-thirty crow-flying miles away, a cere-monial avenue, then the fifty-ton blocks from Marlborough Downs twenty-five miles across the hills . . . weathered, eroded, cracked, broken, leaning, some fallen, many de-stroyed . . . gone . . .

"All great big doorways", whispers the child in us, "and no

44

doors".

The size and numbers are impressive, the weights staggering, the distances formidable, the time it all must have taken beyond our normal comprehension.

According to the latest theories, which change as more is discovered, it was started about two thousand years before the birth of Christ, and completed in about four hundred years. There were, apparently, three main stages in the building . . .

But a detailed knowledge of the confused and speculative archeology is unnecessary to an awareness of the mysteries. It's too easy to lose the meaning in complicated details: not to see Stonehenge for the stones. If you'd like to know more, there are dozens of books and guides . . . but *this* is not about archeology but holiness, the sense of the sacred, feelings not just information: the heart, not the head.

★   ★   ★

However, it all stands inside a circular ditch and double-bank over a hundred yards across, with an entrance facing north-east, the central feature being the two famous concentric stone circles enclosing two horse-shoe rows of larger stones.

Immediately inside the bank there's a circle of fifty-six accurately set small pits, once filled with chalk rubble and now marked with concrete plugs, called the Aubrey Holes, after John Aubrey, the antiquarian who rediscovered them in the seventeenth century. Fragments of human bones and the remains of obvious cremations have been found in them, but the orthodox can only speculate about their function. These pits and the circular ditch were dug about five hundred years before the stone circles were started.

The two outer circles are each of thirty roughly rectangular pillars of extremely hard sandstone called *sarsens,* an obvious corruption of *Saracen.* To the Christian Church of the Middle Ages these circles and megalithic monuments were the work of "Pagans" under the influence of the Devil, and any "heathen" name was good enough to daub them with. "Defend us from Jews, Turks, Infidels, and Heretics". And with the Saracens occupying Jerusalem, the word then stood for everything the Church feared and hated.

Only seventeen of the original thirty sarsens now remain, once supporting a ring of thirty lintels, reduced to six. These lintels link together with tongued-and-grooved joints on their ends, and are held in place by mortices or slots cut into their under surface, which are fitted over tenons or stubs carved on top of each pillar.

In 1954 one of these long since fallen lintels was excavated from centuries of accumulated rubble and earth, and raised to enable it to be more closely examined . . . when it revealed a high level of manual skill and a remarkable feeling for design and sculptural shape. The rubble and earth had preserved it from weathering and vandals, and so it was in much better condition than those still up there on the surviving pillars.

"The sides taper upwards from a flat base", wrote Professor Atkinson, the archeologist in charge of the examination. "All of the edges are slightly curved, and all the surfaces gently rounded, so that the outlines are softened, and the stone takes on a cushioned quality which belies the unyielding hardness of its material. The two mortices . . . are ground smooth and almost polished".

That "taper upwards" of the lintels, and a "slight outward curve" of the pillars, are architectural refinements to "compensate for the effect of perspective" . . . a principle used by the Greeks in the columns of their temples a thousand years later. Otherwise there'd be the "optical illusion" of "narrowing" and instability.

And all this subtle work was done not with chisels of tempered steel but lumps of harder stone used as pounders and grinders.

Within this circle of pillars and lintels is another of sixty smaller standing stones.

Of the two horse-shoe rows inside this, the outer consists of five detached archways (or trilithons) of sarsens, and the inner was originally nineteen stones in a semi-circle with extended arms.

There's a large flat stone near the centre, romantically known as the *Altar*, which is a block of green sandstone from the Cosheston Beds on the shores of Milford Haven at the foot of those Prescelly Mountains. No evidence that it was ever an altar – in fact, it may have once been upright. And there are various other large stones here and elsewhere . . . including the thirty-five ton *Heel Stone,* which stands well outside the main circles near the north-east entrance through the banks and ditch, and is used for sighting on the sun as it rises on Mid-Summer's Day. There's one more slab just inside the bank, which, with a fine touch of melodrama, has been called the *Slaughter Stone* – doubtless on the Christian assumption that all "Pagan" religions went in for human sacrifice and worse.

Again, there's the hand of the Christian Church in that name of the *Heel Stone,* involving a legend about the Devil wanting to do a great work for the bewildering of the world, and so stealing the stones from Ireland – that place again! Well, just as He was arranging them on Salisbury Plain, and boasting to Himself that *now* He'd have the grand puzzling of one and all as to know how the stones came there, a holy friar walked by. "That's more than you can tell", says he to the Devil . . . which enraged Himself. So He chucked a stone at the holy friar, so He did, and hit him on the heel as he was legging away as fast as his two feet would carry him. With the huge impress of the friar's heel to be seen to this day upon that stone, so it is.

A much more likely derivation would be from *helios,* the Greek for sun, as it's the sighting stone.

So there it all is, described in almost totally inadequate words.

*　　*　　*

What's really certain is that the peoples who built it knew how to quarry, hew into shape, transport by land and water, and erect enormous stones weighing up to fifty tons. (Indeed, there's a fallen monolith at Caman in France which is estimated to weigh three-hundred-and-fifty tons). And mathematicians and astronomers have demonstrated that the whole place was laid out in complex patterns of alignment which reveal a considerable detailed knowledge of geometry and astonomy . . . the stones being adjusted into place with an accuracy which modern engineers would be hard pushed to match.

In sobering fact, when the Ministry of Building and Works lifted four of the fallen stones in 1958, using all the latest technology, they couldn't manage it, and left them sixteen inches out of correct horizontal alignment. And, in 1964, they

47

tried again with another fallen stone, setting it in concrete . . . and still got it wrong by several degrees.

Yet those ancient peoples were farmers, apparently with no written language, who did all this heavy and awe-inspiring precision work with rough stone tools, dug with fire-hardened sticks and the antlers of the common red deer, shovelled with the shoulder-blades of oxen, and carted millions of tons of earth and chalk in baskets woven from strips of wattle and leather.

★   ★   ★

How was it all done?

One of the earliest "explanations", and one of the more imaginative, was that of Geoffrey of Monmouth in the twelfth century, whose *Histories of the Kings of Britain* embellishes a legend about Merlin, the High Wizard of King Arthur's Camelot.

Seems that the fifth-century King of Britain, Ambrosius Aurelianus, wanted to commemorate four-hundred-and-sixty Princes and Earls and noble warriors who had recently been treacherously slaughtered by the Saxons under Hengist and Horsa on Salisbury Plain. But his masons couldn't be thinking of a satisfying way of doing this, so what did he do but send for Merlin.

"If thou be fain to grace the burial-place of these men with a work that shall endure for ever", says Merlin, "on Mount Killarus in Ireland there are the Dancing Giants, a structure of stones that none of this age could build", says he. "For these stones be big, nor is there stone anywhere of more virtue, and so", says he, "if they be brought and set up round this place in a circle, here shall they stand for ever. In them is a mystery", says he, "and a healing virtue against many ailments. Giants of old did carry them from the furthest ends of Africa", says he, "and did set them up in Ireland".

And then Merlin led them to "Mount Killarus" in the Kingdom of Ireland, so he did, and "laid the stones down so lightly as none would believe", they all "returned unto Britain with joy", and "there set them up about the compass of the burial-ground". The legend also tells that Merlin "did move the stones" from "Mount Killarus" to Salisbury Plain by his "word

48

of power". And, comments Geoffrey, "proved yet once again how skill surpasseth strength".

Well, as with the stories of St Patrick driving out the snakes from Ireland, behind this legend may be a Folk memory of actual events . . . and which at least gives a grand place a grand origin, so it does.

Mind you, the scientific evidence of geology indicates that none of the stones could possibly have come from Ireland, but that the larger ones came from the Marlborough Downs, about twenty-five miles away, and the smaller ones from outcrops on the Prescelly Mountains of South Wales, a journey by land, sea, river, and land again of at least two-hundred-and-fifty miles.

The great sarsens are sedimentary rocks, weighing fifty tons or more, and at one time they lay all over the Downs like stranded grey whales. Their excavation, shaping, handling, and transportation would have been difficult enough . . . but would have caused nothing like the problems set by the larger number of smaller stones.

These are the so-called bluestones, which are neither intrinsically beautiful nor even all that blue – except when newly fractured. There are at least eighty-two of them, weighing between five and seven tons, they're harder than granite, consist of quartz in crystalline form, make up the inner circle, and are unhewn.

Merely in passing, it's curious to remember that, at least a thousand years later, Moses received special instructions about the use of unhewn stones in worship. "If thou wilt make me an altar of stone", said Jehovah, "thou shalt not build of hewn stone. For if thou lift up a tool upon it, thou hast polluted the stone".

Anyway, there are five separate types of this rock in that inner circle of sixty stones at Stonehenge . . . which are to be found close together in a "spotted dolerite formation" in a small area of those Prescelly Mountains, at Carn Meini, and adjacent outcrops . . . and, according to the geologists, *only* there. And there are hundreds of them still tumbled down the sides of the steep valley.

Which means that they had to be shifted, dragged down the mountain to the Bristol Channel, perhaps floated on rafts along the River Avon to one of its branches, then dragged overland to another river, probably what is now the Hampshire Avon, and finally up the long hill to the site. Two-hundred-and-forty miles of sweating muscle-power, sleds or wooden-rollers, rafts or dug-out canoes, days after day, week after week . . . months . . . years . . .

It's true that the Prescelly Mountains are the nearest source measured in miles, and *we* would probably choose the shortest route to anywhere as obviously the best. But, as we have seen, these ancient peoples didn't work by our standards: time and distance were not so important to them. And so, for all sorts of other reasons, the legend about Merlin and the Dancing Giants of Ireland could equally be true.

The Dancing Giants, remember, were on "Mount Killarus", where they were already set into a circle. Well, "Killarus" is not a surviving place-name in Ireland, but the word may be translated as "the church on the River Ary" – and there *is* a River Ary. Indeed, the famous town of Tipperary gets its name from it. And to the west of the town there are beds of the bluestones, with rivers galore from there to the coast at Waterford. So, as the legend tells, those stones could just as well have been brought from Ireland.

But, from Ireland *or* South Wales, it would have still been a fearful journey, so it would, one we'd think twice or three times about, surely.

Which means that they needed those stones, and none other, for their own special purposes. Precisely *why*, we can only speculate. But it's interesting that they consist of quartz in crystalline form, and *we* use vibrating quartz crystals as atomic clocks, accurate to an umpteenth part of a second over thousands of years. Did *they* know about such vibrations? Remember that non-science isn't necessarily nonsense.

*　　*　　*

Which opens wide the Great Golden Gates into the Technicolored Kingdom.

"Yes", burble the more imaginative dreamers, "it was all a world-wide system for subtle energy transmissions, with Stonehenge acting as a powerful generator requiring exactly those particular stones to function. Alas! such knowledge is now lost to us".

Far-fetched?

Well, with recent advances in "advanced" physics, it would be risky to deny such an idea without a lot of more serious investigation into the "crystal and electro-static properties" of those stones.

Some of the dreamers also suggest that even the fifty-ton sarsens might have been transported and erected by "mental power akin to telekinesis" – or the ability to "move objects at a distance" by the "exertion of thought".

A culture which "may have generated and directed the natural life-giving currents of the earth", write Janet and Colin Bord, "may possibly have developed mental powers which could nullify gravity and manipulate huge masses of stone".

And then there's Ireland in the years of the long ago, where "everyone danced in the air like leaves on the autumn wind", so they did, and "could fly when they sang their songs". So what would be the levitation of a few wee stones to the likes of them?

Which is at least as satisfying as the orthodox archeological notion of our shambling low-browed ancestors doing it all by brute force and barbaric ignorance . . . and so that legend about Merlin using his "word of power" may be another Folk memory of the stones which "hung as it were in the air".

*   *   *

Yet none of that is quite so far-fetched as the established geographical and astronomical alignments of Stonehenge: they range the landscape, yes . . . but they also reach out to the sun, the moon, and the wheeling stars.

As far back as the eighteenth century a "systematic astronomical explanation for the layout" was proposed by Dr John Smith, another enthusiastic antiquarian, who called it a "Lunar Temple", with the stones part of an "elaborate calendar" designed to "match the moon months and the solar year".

In the eighteen-nineties it was suggested by the British astronomer, Sir Norman Lockyer, that one of the purposes of such stone-circles was astronomical: the stones were "markers" used to determine the movements of the sun and moon . . . and,

51

in the early nineteen-sixties, this was confirmed in extraordinary detail when Professor Gerald Hawkins, of the Harvard-Smithsonian Observatory, programmed data about the immense number of possible alignments into a computer (that contemporary minor god), and demonstrated that they could have been used to determine the rising and setting of the sun and moon at different times of the year, the position of certain stars and constellations, and to foretell eclipses of the moon. And Alexander Thom, Professor of Engineering Science at Oxford, has also demonstrated with painstaking thoroughness that many other stone-circles all over the country could have been used in the same way as solar and lunar calendars.

As with the archeology, it's unnecessary to get tangled in the complicated thickets of geometry and astronomy to be impressed: there are books enough to meet the most patient curiosity.

But it's now quite obvious that Stonehenge was the central point of an "incredibly accurate observatory and calculator" which "records the phases of the sun and the cycle of lunar eclipses", and displays a "knowledge of geometry only matched in Classical Greece a thousand years later".

It's perhaps hard to believe when you look at that confusion of standing and fallen stones for the first time – but the truth is that our own short day is measured against the time of the world. Yes, our flesh will die – but the universe abides in those stones.

*　　*　　*

But even that is by no means all.

Because these complex patterns of alignment on features of the landscape and with sun, moon, and the stars "reappear" in the ground-plans of great cathedrals and abbeys of the Middle Ages three thousand years later . . . and are believed by some visionary thinkers to be the real "secrets" of the Masonic Lodges, having to do with focussing the "energies of the solar system" on to these "centres of power", thus "enriching the spiritual life" of the community.

"Nothing less than the complete cosmology of the Ancient World", writes John Michell, "is present entire in the architecture of Stonehenge".

He is an erudite man, deeply read in many a "quaint and curious volume of forgotten lore", a teacher of the Hermetic or Secret Wisdom – exactly the disturbing authority which the orthodox try to dismiss as "dotty" or "loonie" or worse. Yet, for one example, he demonstrates a strange relationship between the "Sacred Geometry" of Stonehenge, the Great Pyramid, the New Jerusalem of the Book of Revelation, and the ground-plan of Glastonbury Abbey.

"Some of these correspondences", he writes, "may be actually invisible to those whose previous knowledge tells them such things cannot exist".

The complete argument is long and difficult, but, to be brutally brief, there are various precise measurements of the New Jerusalem given by St John in the twenty-first chapter of the Book of Revelation: the city "lieth foursquare", and the "length and the breadth and the height of it are equal", being "twelve thousand furlongs". Well, when these and other dimensions are brought to "commensurable proportions", the New Jerusalem can be "identified as a cube containing a sphere, which is in fact a model of the earth on the scale of one foot to one mile".

Now in every Biblical account of the Temple and the Holy City, the "importance of measuring their dimensions is emphasied", and this is "meant literally". For, on this mystical view, the "fabric contains the secrets of the Ancient World set out in such a way that they may be read by anyone in whatever age who cares to undertake the study of the language in which they are written".

True, this language has been neglected, if not wholly lost, but it appears to have been concerned with "images of eternal truth" expressed in numbers and geometrical relationships. "All Things are Numbers", taught Pythagoras. "Number is the Ultimate Reality".

And, of course, in this language the "circle squared" is an obvious symbol of the union of two incommensurable elements, and thus an "image of both man and cosmos", the material and the spiritual. Because the square symbolises the world of solid matter: its perimeter is "precisely and rationally" four times the length of one side. Whereas the circle symbolises spirit, and the measure of its perimeter (or circumference), which is *pi* multiplied by its diameter, can never be defined because of the irrational nature of *pi* . . . a number which could be computed to infinity.

"Square and circle are therefore incommensurate", writes John Michell, "for there is no way of showing that the circumference of a circle is exactly equal to the perimeter of a given square".

Yet the geometrician who tries to "create the true image of the cosmos" must somehow "combine squre and circle of equal perimeter in one scheme of proportion".

And John Michell, though occasionally straining ingenuity, finds this "squaring of the circle" almost everywhere he looks, from Stonehenge to Glastonbury and beyond.

Square the circle of Stonehenge, and you have the four-square New Jerusalem. What does it mean? What sort of mystical truths are supposed to be hidden in these relationships?

That the universe was created by a Divine Intelligence which integrated these relationships into the whole of reality . . . and that the cycle of birth, life, death, decay, and new birth is the base of that reality: as the Moon waxes and wanes, as the Sun rises and sets, so do we.

That we ought to be one with the world, one with the Divine . . . and that wholeness is holiness, healthiness, happiness.

That we survive.

Not much?

Would you say that we are surviving? Are we happy? healthy? happy? Are we whole? at one with the world? Do we any longer believe in anything other than technology? And is that even working?

Will more and more of what is so obviously destroying us ever be our salvation?

Or might it just be possible that we may not even know what the right questions are?

"The past has another pattern . . . we have had the experience but missed the meaning . . ."

*　　*　　*

There's one more mysterious fact: Stonehenge was designed

and built at least two thousand years before St John wrote the Book of Revelation, and yet the same Sacred Geometry appears in both. Which suggests that there is indeed a different order of reality about which most of us know very little, and that Wisdom still "standeth in the top of high places, by the way in the places of the paths . . . at the gates, at the entry of the city . . ."

★   ★   ★

Though there's no shortage of other "explanations" . . .

Stonehenge is "an advanced representation of sepulchral architecture, where the cult of departed ancestors may have become associated with the worship of the Celtic Zeus, under the form of the Sacred Oak".

Again, "considering what magnificence the Romans in prosperous times anciently used in all their works", Inigo Jones concluded that "only they could have built these stately structures", probably as a "Temple dedicated to the Sky God, Coelus".

"This admirable monument", wrote somebody else, "was the burial-place of Queen Boadicea".

Another "conceived this Stupendous Building to have been Erected by the Danes, when they had this Nation in subjection, Design'd to be a Court Royal, or place for the Election and Inauguration of their Kings".

Then, in the seventeenth century, John Aubrey, "with humble submission to better judgements", offered the "probability that it was a Temple of the Druids . . ." And this, despite all the more recent evidence to the contrary, is still the common opinion. Indeed, a contemporary Order of Druids still performs an inauthentic ritual at sunrise on Mid-Summer's Day . . . which, while romantic enough for television, merely obscures the essential mystery. Though it's colourful, and makes a change from *Songs of Praise*.

Some British Israelites see it as one with the Great Pyramid, built by the Lost Tribe of Israel, with its "numerical structure and geometry" as a "preview of Christianity", a "Divine chronometer" giving the "dates of Christ's Nativity and Crucifixion", and a "Prophecy of the future Destiny of

Mankind".

One ingenious theory is that the "building had been designed and built under the direction of an Egyptian colony, the Children of the Sun, established in Britain for political reasons by the High Priests of Ra, the Sun God". Because, runs one of the proofs, "the stone lintels of Stonehenge were carefully shaped to fit the circle they enclosed, the diameter of which, expressed in British inches, is the same diameter of the Egyptian year-circle". The conclusion is "therefore unavoidable" that the circle of Stonehenge is "none other than the Egyptian measure of their Solar Year".

Or its date has been pushed back even further: "The stones had been erected during the days of Adam", and were "knocked down by the Flood".

And there are even claims that it was actually built by the "people of the Lost Continent, Atlantis".

The very lastest ideas are that it's all part of a "world-wide system of co-ordinates" for the "navigational use of Flying-Saucer pilots", or that it's a "storage battery" for "Cosmic Life Forces . . ."

Or something.

Yes, merely the Folklore of True Science, rooted in our anxieties . . .

And yet, and yet . . .

        ★   ★   ★

Because such dreams are the "cause and the measure" of Stonehenge, precisely the sort of release for the creative imagination we most desperately need.

We and our polluted world are obviously on the crumbling edge of catastrophe, largely down to our technology and its dubious assumptions: we have "enslaved the elements", but remain slaves.

The Christian Church has exchanged the living bread of rhapsodic worship for stale crusts of theological chatter, sacrificed the dangerous power of Myth for the scholarly examination of texts, turned the wine back into water. As Theodore Roszak long ago observed: "It has become the religion of the word, not the experience".

But without the soul the dying world is a desert.

56

"Everything that lives is holy", sings William Blake, "life delights in life".

And we have lost the old awe in the face of mysteries.

Yes, we can compute the size of the Universe in light-years, but mistake measurement for understanding . . . and no longer tremble with joy and terror at the heights and depths beyond the stars.

We are now consumer-units, known and numbered . . . and the serpents and wild creatures are driven from us, relegated to zoos and Nature Parks (*Pay at the Gates*) . . . the Sacred Groves have gone for lumber.

And the Moon and the Constellations of the Zodiac only matter in the astrological columns of the popular press and women's magazines.

We mostly lack the feel of the earth around us, wind and wave, soil, rocks, forest, grass and flower and fruit . . . we are rarely in harmony with these forces – and it shows.

Those ancient peoples lived by slower rhythms, months and years rather than the daily demands of time-tables and digital-watches, seasons not split-seconds.

They had a personal relationship with beasts and crops, to eat they killed or cultivated, got blood or dirt on their hands . . . *we* push a trolley along the hygenic racks of a supermarket.

They worshipped the White Goddess with those works and mysteries, marked Her presence among them with great stones . . . *we* bicker about the provisions of the Sunday Trading Act.

To visit Stonehenge is to begin to understand what we lack.

Yes, our food is convenient, preserved, vitamin-enriched, and plastic-wrapped, untouched by human hand. Our recycled water is chemically-purified and fluoridated, our air may be thermostatically-controlled and humidified, our heating central . . . but we are remote from the world.

Television isn't reality.

Come in under the shelter of these rocks.

Something survives of those who brought them there: conviction, knowledge . . . mystery . . .

THE PREGNANT EARTH MOTHER

While you are anywhere near Stonehenge you must extend your awareness of the Great Mother in the landscape by climbing the Hill of Silbury.

This is sixteen or so miles to the north, and is described in the guide-books as the "largest man-made structure in Europe" – as though women had no part in its purpose or making.

The mere facts and figures are, as usual, more astonishing than all the possible "explanations" about its purpose.

As John Michell points out, it's "a noted centre for alignments of dead-straight prehistoric tracks . . . and of standing stones, and several churches on ancient sites". And Michael Dames has demonstrated that it is also "aligned with solstitial and equinoctial events". Though there is far more to the place than that.

By the evidence of radio-carbon dating it was probably built about two-thousand-seven-hundred years before the birth of Christ, slightly earlier than the first pyramids of Egypt.

The Hill is an enormous mound covering five-and-a-half acres, one-hundred-and-thirty feet high, a diameter of over a hundred feet across its flat top, constructed with chalk dug from an apparently irregular ditch partly surrounding it . . . over nine million cubic feet, dug with those picks and shovels of wood and bone, and carted with those baskets of wattle and leather.

And not just roughly heaped and pounded into shape, or simply dug and piled like a modern industrial tip, because recent archeological work has revealed the method of construction. Its foundations were started on a natural outcrop of chalk, the ground-plan laid out methodically with large blocks of chalk as a retaining wall, and then "carefully engineered" with "carved chalk blocks" in a series of "concentric rings" of "stepped horizontal layers" or courses, with a progressive filling-in of rubble as the work mounted upwards.

And even the Romans, when they came two-thousand-five-hundred years later, respected its mere bulk enough to "turn aside" the straight road they were building from Silchester through Speen to Bath.

There aren't any obvious graves or burial-chambers inside, and the orthodox have no evidence and little idea about its purpose. Most of them regard it as a Bronze-Age barrow, merely a mound of earth raised above a burial-chamber they haven't yet managed to discover ... though there *are* these legends about King Sil being buried at its heart, and him in full armour, a life-size figure of solid gold, either on the back of his fine horse, or lain in a golden coffin. True, the archeologists freely admit that it's far larger than any other barrow ... but, er, what *else* can it possibly be?

As with the Heel Stone at Stonehenge, there's the hand of the Christian Church in the attempt to "explain" it away by legends.

For example, not even the Devil could put up with the Pagan religion at Avebury a mile or three up the road, so He planned to drop a load of earth on it and have done with such blasphemy ... but it slipped out of a hole in the bottom of the sack, so it did, and landed at Silbury. And other versions tell how it was Marlborough or Devizes He was planning to cover, but was prevented by St John – who just happened to be passing at the time.

And there are all manner of stories about spectacular thunder-storms which break over it during archeological excavations ... evidence of the "superstitious dread" in which it is still held locally.

But, the Devil's sack aside, on all the usual terms, careful, scholarly, even fastidious, it remains baffling ...

Within it lies hidden the secrets of time before history.

★   ★   ★

But in the world of the imagination, in the necessary language of fire and roses, the Hill of Silbury is a most evocative and strangely moving feature of the Sacred Landscape in which our ancestors worked out their myths and dreams.

For instance, it's been described as "a gigantic sun-dial to determine the Seasons and the true length of the year", with references to the Zodiac and Glastonbury, with it "used as an accurate solar observatory by means of the shadow cast on the carefully levelled plain to the north".

And Michael Dames, in an enthralling book, *The Silbury Treasure,* subtitled *The Great Goddess Rediscovered,* suggests that we can see this "primordial hill" as "the womb of a pregnant woman" immediately before giving birth.

The idea begins with that apparently irregular ditch.

In fact, this is an intricate system of ring-walls around a moat, forming an artificial lake channelled with water from the River Kennet which meanders past from its nearby source. To this day the system is often flooded . . . and, from above, resembles a *sheelagh-na-gig* – a woman squatting with her thighs parted in the traditional (as opposed to our contemporary male-dominated flat-on-the-back) delivery position for natural birth.

The *sheelagh-na-gig* is an ancient fertility figure of a naked woman squatting to display her exaggeratedly large genitals, often opening the vaginal lips even wider with her fingers, while looking straight at the spectator as though challenging response . . . staring with exactly the same sort of eyes as those of the Earth Mother discovered by T. C. Lethbridge in the chalk of the Gogmagog Hills. She's obviously the feminine counterpart to such male images of unashamed potency as the Cerne Abbas Giant with his disproportionately large erection . . . but, surprisingly, though starkly Pagan, she's still to be found in many early Irish, Saxon, and Norman churches, carved on capitals or grinning among the gargoyles, and thus mysteriously incorporated into Christian worship. True, many have been defaced or destroyed, yet enough survive to demonstrate not only her elemental power but the pragmatic ability of the Church to absorb ideas so radically opposed to its own negative views about women and their "dangerous" sexuality.

The name *sheelagh-na-gig* is usually translated from the Old Irish as "Sheila of the Paps", though in most of them the breasts are rarely emphasised, even rudimentary, and the word is probably a corruption of *Sithlach-na-gig*, "Holy Lady of the Gods", or "Mother of the Gods" . . . which would be much more in harmony with Her unmistakable functions.

And a few miles away from Silbury the Parish church of Winterbourne Monkton has a stone font, with the Great Mother as a *sheelagh-na-gig* "giving birth to the vegetation of the earth".

So, with all this in mind, Michael Dames goes on to suggest that the Hill of Silbury "was the scene of a Stone-Age religious rite", an essential part of their agricultural year. For, at the beginning of our August, on the last of the four annual festivals of the Pagan year, when the corn was ripe for cutting, the people would "climb to the terrace just below the summit" and "watch the Goddess giving birth".

The moon rises over Waden Hill, the "light falls across the thighs of the woman and illuminates the vaginal entrace". And then, at about eleven-thirty, the moon is reflected in the moat . . . which may be seen as "the baby's head emerging from between the woman's thighs". A few hours later the light "falls on her breast, and the reflection of the moon in the water simulates flowing milk". The "child is now suckling", the birth is safely complete, the woman is now a mother . . . and the corn can be harvested.

Silbury is a Hill of Harvest and Birth.

The orthodox are understandably embarrassed at the whole idea . . . but it's interesting that this Pagan festival remains a "feast" of the Church as Lammas: Loaf Mass, the offering of the first-fruits, a celebration of the first bread baked from the new grain of the harvest – at that same beginning of August. And, on Palm Sunday, until quite recently, the villagers from nearby Avebury used to climb the Hill of Silbury to "eat fig-cakes and drink water sweetened with sugar". Figs are, of course, an almost universal symbol of fecundity, the tree combining both masculine and feminine principles in the leaf and fruit . . . with the sweet water perhaps a Folk memory of mother's milk.

What, indeed, could be more holy and healthy than birth? What more worthy of worship or "worth-giving" than motherhood?

And to walk along the lanes of Wiltshire, by fields of ripening wheat, and see that great pregnant belly of earth swelling in the landscape is to be moved by memories of your own mother, your own birth, your own nine-month journey from the depths of her womb to the unknown world . . . to experience the tiding of the waters, the struggle of change, the newness of breath, the urgency to move beyond the warm comfort of safe constriction into the chilling freedom, the terror of life and all manner of other magnificence.

*　　*　　*

61

Past, present, and future, then – these three.

The past is remembrance of that Lost Kingdom, or the nightmare of history. The moment now is the only time, here on that belly, your lips at the milky nipple . . . a young lover's glimpse of the mystery. And the future is a smell of baking bread, the first of the harvest, a promise of wine in the ripening grapes . . . seeds of life in the aching tomb.

But *now* is the Season of Wheat and Roses, through *this* Night the Moon climbs . . . each new day the sun arises.

Surely, this is holy ground.

AVEBURY RING

Just north of Silbury, this is the largest of the thousand or more stone circles that either survive or are known to have existed in Britain. Even older than Stonehenge, and three times larger – so obviously an important religious site: a huge and sprawling structure of three stone circles, two processional avenues approaching it from either side in sweeping curves, an enormous and steep-sided circular bank and ditch, thirty feet deep and over four hundred yards in diameter, nearly a mile in circumference, enclosing twenty-eight acres, sixty great stones in two circles, another hundred in a larger circle around them, forty-ton sarsens of intractable sandstone, a few of them even larger, twenty-five feet high, sixty tons . . . awe-inspiring . . .

Again, the facts and figures are ultimately meaningless, of importance only to those obsessed by measurement. And this is not about steel tapes or theodolites, but the mystery of holiness.

And Avebury is undoubtedly both mysterious and holy.

*   *   *

It's at the far end of a gentle valley, almost surrounded by the Downs, and there are dozens of small barrows scattered all over the area . . . with a view of the Hill of Silbury behind you.

John Aubrey, whose name was given to that circle of fifty-six holes at Stonehenge, visited Avebury for the first time at Christmas in 1648, and returned again and again, fascinated and disturbed by the vision of these great stones. And it is to this civilised and curious man, whose *Brief Lives* is one of the delights of English Literature, that we owe most of our knowledge of what he called "this stupendous antiquity" and its condition before it was destroyed. "Avebury", he wrote, "doth as much exceed in greatness the so renowned Stonehenge in grandeur as a Cathedral doeth an ordinary Parish Church".

He actually made quite a careful survey of both Stonehenge and Avebury, and wrote an extraordinarily interesting account of his many discoveries at the genial command of Charles the Second, and eventually compiled the *Monumenta Britannica*, a vast and disorderly miscellany about earthworks and barrows, castles and funerary urns, sepulchres and Roman Roads, with copious quotations from Homer, the Venerable Bede, Sir Thomas Browne, and dozens of other equally "curious" writers. And came to the conclusion that it was all a *Templa Druidum* . . . "by its grandeur one might presume it to have been an Arch-Temple of the Druids" . . . being the "most eminent Order of Priests among the Britains".

Mind you, it is now difficult to "see" the place as it once was, because the village of Avebury has been built within the site, and the stones circle around and between the cottages and streets. Indeed, almost all of its stones have been smashed and looted for walls – with some of the cottages obviously built from them.

First, the Christian Church did its best to desecrate the place. Part of the bank was shovelled into the ditch in the fourteenth century, and most of the sarsens were over-thrown. And then, in the eighteenth century, local farmers and landowners carried on the destruction, cracking them by fire and water for building-stone and rubble for roads . . . what William Stukely, yet another enthusiastic antiquarian, called "these acts of wretched ignorance and avarice". For over thirty years this man of wide culture and scholarship had to watch helplessly as they "toppled and smashed the great stones", though he did all he could to make "careful drawings and measurements" to preserve knowledge of the place. One stone he described as being "at the centre" was over twenty-five feet tall. He named this the "obelisk" . . . but it's long since been destroyed.

And it was William Stukely who first recognised the presence of the ancient Solar Serpent there.

Anyway, as at the Hill of Silbury, the main ditch was

originally filled with water channelled from the River Kennet, thus making the site a holy island. On this were the hundred immense sarsens and the two smaller circles, all mostly desecrated . . . so that now there are "only a few stray monoliths in the fields and cottage-gardens of the village".

It's interesting to note that in the Great Circle, as well as in the surviving remains of the two avenues, the stones are alternately tall pillars and squat diamond-shapes . . . which may be male and female symbolism. Yes, once you start looking, it's possible to suspect a Freudian phallus in every tower, an archetypal vagina in every innocent church-porch – but sometimes such symbols were intended for all the world to see . . . though others have seen these alternating stones as "representations of the Goddess as the Virgin and the Pregnant Woman".

Beyond the Great Circle there are remains and traces of the two processional avenues, fifteen yards wide and each over a mile-and-a-half long, lined on either side by what used to be hundreds and hundreds of sandstone boulders.

One avenue curves away to the south-east, down into the dip of the valley, then up, and ends on the flat top of a low hill in a small double stone circle called the Sanctuary. The other makes a "sinuous double curve" to the south-west, and William Stukely noted that both together they may be seen as the Solar Serpent, with the Sanctuary representing the head, and the avenues forming the body – which intersects what could be the Sun Disc of Avebury Ring.

"These symbols of the Solar Disc and the Serpent were used to express the highest ideals", write Janet and Colin Bord, "those of the Supreme Creative Being, and the wisdom of inner truths".

A strange fact connected with this Serpent in the landscape of Avebury is that there's a twelfth-century stone font in the Parish church, carved with a winged serpent biting the foot of a bishop – who is striking its head with the end of his staff. Which, as with St Patrick, seems to be an obvious symbolic reference to the "battle" between the old "Solar Serpent" worship and the new Christianity. Indeed, Avebury was traditionally "one of the more resistant centres" to the "upstart" religion, and the seventh-century Saxon church, instead of assuming a dominant position within the circle like so many other churches, was built outside the western bank of the Ring, and well away from the centre of the village.

An equally strange fact is that the Sanctuary, or head of the Serpent, is on the southern end of a ridge called Hackpen Hill . . . with "hac" the Old English name for serpent, and "pen" meaning head: Serpent Head.

And, as we have seen, John Michell points out that "one of the longest and most important" ley-lines in the whole of Britain passes through Avebury Ring on its way from St Michael's Mount to the North Sea.

It's also been suggested that the earliest part of the vast Avebury complex is the long barrow at West Kennet, a burial chamber constructed of giant sarsens . . . which could be seen as the White Goddess as the Hag or Crone of Death. Then, with the Hill of Silbury as the Goddess of Harvest giving birth, Avebury thus becomes the Goddess as the Virgin Bride in the place of conception . . . the whole area being a part of the Sacred landscaping.

And Evan Hadingham, a most serious and restrained writer, with many reservations, admits that it's "easy" to "imagine a multitude of Druidically-robed priests with arms outstretched . . . religious chantings . . . the solemn pacing of a funeral procession . . ."

So, if they're right, there was something mysterious going on there, and, for all the desecration and destruction, it's the most impressive religious site in the country . . . large enough to embrace the village, and yet retain the sense of vastness and ancient significance.

Beautiful in its own way, a living landscape, changing from hour to hour, season to season, yet always strangely the same . . . contrasts, shadows, vistas, sheep and cattle safely grazing, new grass and old stone . . . purposes we can only wonder at . . .

Come early in the morning, perhaps when there are mists about, or stay until late twilight . . . and allow the stones to loom and shift in the landscape of your imagination, let time drift . . . the moon to rise . . . dream . . .

"Whose are those voices?"

Yes, the best history remains unwritten . . . for *us* to write it.

There are many other such mysterious stone circles and mounds and barrows all over Britain, at any one of which you could come into touch with powers and movements of the soul that will transform your ways of seeing, stir your imagination . . . reveal another and more significant order or reality than that of headlines and troubles and great tribulations . . . signs, wonders . . .

For one, part of the whole Avebury complex is that West Kennet long barrow, which can be seen as the White Goddess in Her terrible aspect as the Hag or Crone of Death. It's just east across from the Hill of Silbury, a short walk over the fields or round by the lanes: a great packed heap of earth and chalk more than three hundred feet in length and ten feet high, covering a large structure of drystone interior walling. There are enormous gnarled sarsens as portal stones, almost gargoyles, an entrance literally as dark as the mouth of the grave, a low passage into the tomb or womb, more great stones . . . several chambers . . . silence, the utter silence of four-thousand-four-hundred years . . . hardly the sound of your own heart beating . . .

Is this death? Or are you waiting for birth?

To come back out into the weather is its own answer.

*   *   *

Or there's Castle Rigg, in Cumbria, a mile or so east of Keswick, a wind-swept stone circle surrounded by the Lakeland Fells, Derwent Water to the south, Skiddaw to the north, "the homes of the silent vanished races" . . . the changing clouds, the chasing shadows . . . yes, even the landscape will bring you peace, inspiration, health . . .

*   *   *

Or, by that "distant northern sea", there's the strangely beautiful chambered tomb of Maes Howe, at the southern end of Loch Harray, up on the Mainland of Orkney . . . "one of the greatest works of architecture" in Britain, says William Anderson. The whole area is rich with tombs and monuments, standing stones and mysteries – but Maes Howe is unique.

All it is from the outside is a rough mound of clay and stones about twenty-five feet high . . . but deep inside is a stooping passage over thirty feet long, lined with enormous slabs of sandstone, leading to a square stone chamber fifteen feet across, with the corbelled roof arching over in precise elegance. This roof is a marvel, each thin course of stone projecting slightly beyond the one below, layer on layer, stepping higher and higher, everything balanced and solid . . . pyramidical . . .

"It has a startlingly contemporary look", says Evan Hadingham, "almost as if it were designed by a modern architect".

And there's that same utter silence, unheard music, the tides of blood roaring in your ears . . . another sea at the "naked shingles of the world".

★   ★   ★

And when you emerge, there, across the way, on a narrow strip of land between Loch Stennes and Loch Harray, is the Ring of Brodgar, the most dramatic of holy places: twenty-seven standing stones, tall, slender, stark against the sky. Used to be sixty, but the others have long since been destroyed for all the usual miserable reasons. Enclosed by a bank and ditch, almost a quarter-of-a-mile around, various alignments on the rising of the moon . . . runic inscriptions left by the Vikings, a few by early Irish travellers . . .

But those weathered stones, hooded, looming, sometimes menacing . . .

What are they saying?

Have we even got the humility to listen?

★   ★   ★

Or Callanish, another ring of thirteen great slender white stones beside Loch Roag on the Isle of Lewis in the Outer Hebrides. It's a remote place, austere, deserted, difficult to reach . . . which means that only those who make the effort will come there, so you may be alone under that wide sky . . . clouds for company . . . thoughts . . .

Loch Roag is a long narrow inlet sheltered from the Atlantic by a low promontory of rocky land, though there's nearly always that Western wind, the presence of the pounding sea . . . and it's as though the tall stones are really the petrified trunks of a geometrical grove of sacred trees. Because they're grained, textured, knotted, gnarled, with long cracks, all seemingly rooted in the earth, growing from it. There's a central pillar, a small burial cairn, a long avenue of standing stones, an outcrop of great boulders, other chambered cairns, several more megalithic sites within view . . . alignments on sunrise and sunset . . . the Moon, the Pole Star . . .

Time beyond time, unknown purposes . . .

Weep a while, perhaps, and then be silent.

*   *   *

Or Spiral Castle at Brugh-na-Boyne . . . now called New Grange.

Now wouldn't *that* be in Ireland, surely?

On the east coast, by the banks of a bend in the River Boyne, six miles west of Drogheda, so it is, the finest of all chambered tombs, finished a thousand years before Stonehenge was even started . . . a vast hump shouldering like a stranded grey whale over at the top of a field, thirty feet high, a quarter-of-a-mile around, great slabs of rock ringing the base, some incised with double spirals and geometrical shapes, the whole faced by blocks of white quartz, an all-over pattern of embedded sea-rounded boulders, with quartz and boulders carted many miles from the coast . . . two-hundred-thousand tons of stone . . . ten enormous herms, eight tons or more, in a semi-circle at the southern end . . . another hundred set edge to edge ringing the place . . .

Yes, all the usual incomprehensible sizes and weights . . .

There's a squared dolmen portal, with what's been called a "light box" over the lintel, and, on the ground in front of the entrance, an immense stone carved and incised with a maze of spirals and circles like snakes, like serpents, the waves of the sea, like nothing at all on the face of the living earth.

Then in you go, down a long passage lined with huge slabs of stone, plenty of head-room, more spirals and circles, down to the spacious chamber at the far end, twenty feet high, three recesses like chapels, the roof a corbelled bee-hive . . . and there, on the back wall, facing the entrance, another three patterns of twining whorls and spirals . . . snakes? mazes? eddies of water? eyes? forked lightning? electromagnetic lines of force? or what else in the world?

Well, when the place was excavated and restored in the late nineteen-sixties, it was discovered (as who could doubt?) that the long passage was so aligned that the light of sunrise on the Winter Solstice passes through that light-box over the lintel, illuminates the back wall . . . and for a few minutes after dawn, makes those spirals live . . .

"Follow the lines with your finger from outside to inside", wrote Robert Graves, "and when you reach the centre there is the head of another spiral coiled in the reversed direction to take you out of the maze again. So the pattern typifies death and rebirth . . ."

For the Sun has died, sunk in the southern sky to the lowest depths, and swung to the furthest east in His daily rising. But now the Solstice is here and passing, each new day the Sun will now rise higher and warmer towards the glories of High Summer . . . because the rays at *this* dawn penetrate into the heart of the mound, into the womb of the Great Mother – and from *Her* will be born all good and necessary things.

So the place is not only one of the largest burial mounds ever constructed, every lump of which had to be carted there by human labour, but also a deliberate and symbolic astronomical clock which recorded the Sacred Time of the Winter Solstice . . . when the Consort of the Great Mother began His rebirth from the Spiral Castle of Winter and Death. With the use of white quartz confirming the dedication to the White Goddess, Custodian of the Dead.

Perhaps it was more than a tomb and womb, but also a place of initiation where you would be subjected to the deepest forms of terror: the darkness of panic, the plunge into Hell, the eternity of death without hope . . . and, if you survived, you'd emerge again into the light of day, inspired with wisdom . . . assured of new and everlasting life . . .

Anyway, according to legends, and them as true as the grass is green, it was said to have been the home of the Dagda Himself,

Son of Bridget, the High One or Triple Goddess . . . and the High Kings of Ireland were buried here – and why wouldn't they be?

*　　*　　*

So as with Stonehenge and nearly every other holy place, go with your standard guide-book and loaded camera, and all you'll be impressed by is the size of the place, the strangeness, the number of other tourists milling around looking for the loo.

But give yourself time, see as a child or pilgrim, enter into the spirit of those who built it . . . and you'll be aware of terror and death, the hope of rebirth, the renewal of life and the earth, the promise of Spring and Harvest to come.

For wasn't Ireland holy ground long before St Patrick set foot on it?

Sacred Waters and Woods

After the Age of Stone came the Ages of Bronze and Iron, tools, weapons, wars, technology . . . and in came the Celts and their kings: tall, blue-eyed, red-headed.

"To the frankness and high-spiritedness of their temperament", wrote Strabo, the Roman historian, "must be added the traits of childish boastfulness and love of decoration. They wear ornaments of gold, torcs on their necks, and bracelets on their arms and wrists, while people of high rank wear dyed garments besprinkled with hasps of gold. It is this vanity which makes them unbearable in victory and so completely downcast in defeat. In addition to their witlessness they possess a trait of barbarian savagery . . ."

Vain, restless, quarrelsome . . . didn't they dare to sack Rome itself in the early days of the long ago?

True, they also had noble qualities: "If the brown leaves falling in the woods were gold", sang one Irish Bard in praise of the great Finn Mac Cumhal, "if the white waves were silver, he would have given away the whole of it".

And why wouldn't he, being Irish?

They started coming from Central Europe a thousand years before Christ was born, warriors rather than farmers, tamers and riders of horses, invaders rather than migrants . . . and they brought swords into the old matriarchial society: agression.

Once there had been harmony, men and women working together, each doing what they did best, with womanly virtues held to be sacred, paramount . . . the Great Mother was Queen of Heaven, the Sun Her Consort.

Now the loud-mouthed warriors strutted and swaggered, kings wore crowns of gold to their arrogant heads . . . and the women were eventually regarded as biddable enough creatures for the bed and kitchen.

"The balance was upset", says William Anderson, "with consequences that are still to be put right today".

And the typical works of the Celts were their forts, gigantic defensive enclosures, banks and ditches and high walls of tree-trunks around the tops of hills: hundreds of them, all over the country.

The Venerable Bede, who was writing when many of them must still have been in good repair, describes one he believed to be Roman as "constructed with lumps cut from the earth and raised above ground level, fronted by the ditch from which the lumps were cut, and surmounted by a strong palisade of logs".

Some were spectacular: Maiden Castle in Dorset, for instance, is a mile-and-a-half around, and encloses over one-hundred-and-twenty acres, with a series of four deep ditches and steep earth-walls sixty feet high . . . which it took all the iron might of Vespasian and his Legions to storm when he conquered the south-west.

Yet it was never a holy place, surely?

Like many of our contemporary weapons, aircraft-carriers, supersonic jet-bombers, nuclear-rockets, these hill-forts may be impressive, awe-inspiring, often beautiful . . . but nothing dedicated to death can be truly holy.

The ancient peoples of this country climbed to the hills because they were sacred . . . the new invaders retreated there to feel safe from their mortal enemies.

True, the Celts may not have constructed all of these forts, and probably adapted many existing earth-works – but it was as forts they used them.

However, there *were* sanctuaries, holy places . . .

★   ★   ★

"Springs, wells and rivers", writes Anne Ross, Herself an authority on most things Celtic, "are of first and enduring importance as a focal point of their cult practice and ritual".

Yes, springs and streams have always been holy places, obviously symbols of life and fertility and the beneficence of the Great Mother . . . and in them we still have a shiver of contact with ancient times.

"A garden inclosed is my Sister, my Spouse", sings the Lover in the *Song of Songs*, "a spring shut up, a fountain sealed . . . a fountain of gardens, a well of living waters, and streams from Lebanon".

And, as Aubrey Burl remarks in his book, *The Stone Circles of the British Isles,* "Where an avenue of stones is associated with a

72

stone circle it almost invariably leads from a source of water, indicating the importance of water in the ceremonies that took place at the rings" . . . with Stonehenge the prime example, so close to the River Avon.

Old stones will speak if you listen, but living waters will always sing . . . and the Celts sang with them, and gave the names of their Gods and Goddesses to the rivers they found here: the Thames, the Dee and the Clyde, the Severn, the Wharfe, the Braint of Anglesey and the Brent of Middlesex, the Boyne and the Shannon of Ireland . . . and they venerated them for their giving of life, their strength, their powers of destruction. And they worshipped by throwing in votive offerings, rings and coins of gold, weapons, shields, pottery, drinking-cups of embossed silver, and all manner of other treasures . . . even making them specifically for use as such offerings.

Pools and lakes were also venerated and worshipped in this way, but wells and springs were apparently their most sacred places. Indeed, they were great diggers of shafts, and many have been discovered – though, of course, many more must have been lost over the centuries. Some are square, some circular, some are obviously wells for the extraction of domestic water – but some are probably ritual shafts having to do with symbolic entrance to the Other World. One of these, at Wilsford in Wiltshire, two miles from Stonehenge, the entrance in a burial-mound, was over a hundred feet deep in the chalk . . . and another, near Dunstable, is closer to a hundred-and-twenty feet, and was filled with human and animal bones, sandstone altar-slabs, pottery, tiles, charred wood, and coins – an apparent mixture of burials, sacrifices, and offerings.

Anne Ross describes a particularly interesting Celtic well at Ashill in Norfolk, square, lined with wood, and forty feet deep. In the upper twenty feet or so they found broken pottery, bones, the staves of a wooden bucket, the remains of a wickerwork basket, an iron knife, and all that sort of household rubbish. But below this there were "fairly perfect urns placed in layers, and embedded in leaves of hazel and hazel nuts" – the significance of these being that the "hazel tree was venerated" and had a "traditional association with sacred wells". Because the Well of Segais in the Celtic Land of Promise was the "source of all knowledge", surrounded by hazel trees, with the ripe nuts falling in the water and "producing bubbles of inspiration".

And there are the remains of a small Temple built over such a Sacred Well at Carrawbrough in Northumberland, close to a later Roman fort and Temple of Mithras. It was dedicated to Coventina, a Celtic fertility Goddess of triple aspect, Virgin Bride, Mother, and Crone of the Dead ... and more than fourteen-thousand coins, votive offerings in bronze, brooches, pottery, and shrine-bells were recovered from it during excavations at the end of the nineteenth century. This well is still there, but surrounded by marshy land, so you can't really get close except at the end of a week or so of dry weather.

Unfortunately, as Anne Ross goes on to point out, these Temples or Shrines were of the "simplest kind", usually "wooden frames and wickerwork", or "wattle and daub walls" . . . and they leave "little trace after their destruction".

True, during the later Roman invasions, some of these wells and springs, especially the thermal and mineral ones, were taken over, enlarged and elaborated, and incorporated into the religious and social life of the Roman community.

Bath, for example, was known as *Aquae Sulis*, the Waters of Sulis, a Celtic Goddess, who, in typical Roman practicality, was assimilated with Minerva, "invoked in Her theraputic capacity" – with the place used as a hospital and convalescent camp for sick or wounded legionaries. And, again, Buxton in Derbyshire was known as *Aquae Arnemetiae*, the Waters of Arnemetia, another Celtic Goddess . . . and the "waters" of both places are famous to this day.

Neither of the two Roman pools at Buxton survive in their original state, but there are bits and pieces of the once magnificent Temple of Sulis Minerva still to be seen at Bath . . . and the main pool is still there. However, for all the nineteenth-century restorations, it's almost impossible to experience any of the ancient awe there . . . "The world is too much with us", too many people, too many shops and cars and noise. If Proteus or old Triton rose from *those* waters they'd be blinded by a battery of instantaneous photo-flashes.

*   *   *

There are, of course, thousands of ancient Holy Wells all over the landscape, from Aberdeen and Anglesey to Warwickshire and Wiltshire by way of Northumberland, Pembroke, and most points in several directions . . . with Ireland wet underfoot with them, surely. Wouldn't you be hard pushed to cross from Dublin to Galway, or from Cork up to Derry, without passing more Holy Wells than breweries?

St Patrick led the way, from Tyrone to Mayon, baptising and healing, closely followed by St Brigid and two-thirds of the Calendar of Irish Saints . . . with most of the places still more Pagan than Christian: such walking barefoot through the shallows and traipsing three times sunwise around the well-head, so many pebbles added to the heaps already there or taken away with a quick spit and a quicker prayer, so many wee bits of rag or clean handkerchiefs tied to so many whitethorn trees, dropping in the coins . . . and why wouldn't anybody be taking the three sips or the seven from the clear springing water?

Indeed, at one famous Shrine I've even seen a Roman Catholic priest take a swig to be washing down a couple of asprin.

Though be warned: you may be disappointed, for you can hear tell of some famous Holy Waters, and travel there over many miles of rough roads and tracks, eventually trace it . . . and, in the words of Hill Burton, a determined nineteenth-century seeker, "find a tiny spring bubbling out of the rock, such as you may see hundreds of in a tolerable walk any day".

The rest of Britain, being that much less Celtic, takes its wells more sedately, even solemnly . . . and you'll find them railed-in and preserved in the most surprising corners, next to the car-park, with an explanatory notice and convenient litter-bin. And, a sad mark of their decline, usually turned into Wishing Wells, with a discreet wire-mesh for the easier collection of the hopeful coins.

True, some remain impressive . . .

★   ★   ★

One of the oldest, probably going back two thousand years, is at Golant, a couple of miles north of Fowey in Cornwall, close to the river. It's next to the church, St Sampson's – a dedication which probably has more to do with a nod in the direction of the nearest Pagan Giant the like of the one at Cerne Abbas than any Christian saint. Used to be a hermit's cell there in the sixth century, so it was already holy then.

And isn't there St Augustine's Well at Cerne Abbas itself? with him supposed to have struck the ground with his staff for the water to gush. Not a decent stone's throw from the Giant, through the churchyard, and down along a cobbled track between the lime trees . . . with that well having as much to do with any saint's staff as that club in the right hand of the Big Lad up there on the hill.

At the head of Ullswater, up in Cumbria, St Patrick was obviously about again . . . and even though the well is by the side of the main road the water is worth a stop.

There's a lovely one in the Forest of Dean, St Anthony's, north of Cinderford, close by Plump Hill, where you follow the sound of running water through the wood . . . and what better way to be finding a well? And with it having a small bathing pool, marvellously cold, especially on high days of Summer . . . so, if there's nobody else about, why not take a quick trip back to the Garden of Eden? The legend is that it'll cure you of any diseases of the skin – and why wouldn't it? Be there at the rising of the sun in the Merry Month of May, and be baptising yourself the nine times. There's health and wholeness for you! Unless you prefer the National Health Service?

According to Janet and Colin Bord, the "most active Holy Well in England, probably in Britain", is at the High Anglican Shrine of Our Lady of Walsingham. Unlike Lourdes, She was never actually there Herself, but a hundred-thousand pilgrims a year pay their respects . . . and you're more than welcome to join them. The church is recent, vaguely Byzantine, the statues are romantically Medieval, and the built-in well is at the foot of a few marble steps on the left as you enter. However, it must be said that the Holy Well at Walsingham in the Middle Ages was across the road, hard by the now ruined Augustinian Priory . . . but what's a hundred yards in matters of faith?

*   *   *

A slightly more authentic experience of a pilgrimage may be had at the equally famous St Winefride's Well at Holywell in Flint,

North Wales. It's just below the church, there's an ornate stone chapel over the well, a statue of the saint, and a small open-air bathing-pool outside.

Winefride, the beautiful and virginal daughter of an eighth-century Welsh chieftain, "resisted the advances" of Prince Caradoc, who "struck off her head with his sword" . . . and where her head fell "water gushed from the earth". Her murderer was immediately "cursed" by her uncle, St Beuno, so that he died in agony on the spot, and she was miraculously healed, with the "thin white scar on her throat" to mark her escape, the well to bear witness to the miracle, and other signs to follow.

"The drops of her blood", sang Tudur Aled, a Welsh Bard, "are as the red shower of the berries of the wild rose, the tears of Christ from the height of the Cross".

Which is a magnificent image for any believer, surely?

And the red moss which still grows on the stones is said to represent her blood-stained hair – another lovely image . . . and the legend has it that for three days after her eventual death the well produced milk, or at least a "milk-like fluid" murmur the prudent.

However, Celtic Mythology is so rich in these legends of wells springing at places where severed heads had either fallen or been buried, the presumption must be that behind this story there's probably the presence of an ancient well dedicated to the Great Goddess whose breasts sustained the earth, which had been assimilated into Christian hagiography at an early date. It's obviously been rebuilt or restored several times, with most the present structure about four hundred years old, arches and leaded windows and imitation battlements. The water is claimed to cure all manner of diseases, and to grant fertility – another sign of a more ancient origin . . . and many pilgrims still come every year to drink or bathe in search of help. Unfortunately, "mining operations have diverted the spring", and the well is now "serviced" by a local reservoir . . . possibly with some effect on the number of cures. An admission charge is made, which, as always, does a lot to destroy any genuine feelings of holiness.

Yet the holy truth is not easily denied, and people *have* been moved there . . . Gerard Manley Hopkins for instance. He spent three years studying at the Jesuit College of St Beuno, which is only six or so miles away, and he and a friend walked over the hills, bathed there, and "returned very joyously". In fact, the sight of the water "as clear as glass, greenish like beryl or aquamarine, trembling at the surface with the force of the springs", inspired him, and he actually began a verse tragedy about St Winefride.

So, yes, something lingers . . .

⋆   ⋆   ⋆

And at Glastonbury in Somerset there's Chalice Well, right at the foot of the Tor, with the water having a slight reddish tinge. "Ah!" says the legend, "that's from the Sacred Blood of Christ which still flows from the Holy Cup used at the Last Supper, with it buried under the hill by St Joseph of Aramathea those long years ago". Anyway, Chalice Well is in a garden, "to which an admission charge is payable".

Which is a problem as old as Christianity.

"Oh! the vast sums of money that are gotten by such trade", said George Fox once and for all, "notwithstanding the Scriptures were given forth freely . . ."

As freely, indeed, as the waters of well and springs, surely.

⋆   ⋆   ⋆

So, as ever and always, make your own way, have eyes to see the silver flashings of the sun on a distant stream in the green shade of a wood, have ears for that sound of running water . . . and find your own spring, your own well, your own wholeness at a place of peace.

Beneath the roots of trees, burbling and babbling from fissures in the tumbled rocks, there'll be that deep down freshness somewhere, that clear coldness. Watch it welling, then, filling the channel, flowing away . . . from what secret depths? Feel the "force that drives the water through the rocks", listen to the song it sings, "whirl the water in the pool", bathe your hands and face, enjoy the gentle shock . . . taste . . . and know the place as sacred, the time as holy.

But, whatever you do, don't throw anything in there . . . not

78

even as an offering.

Because aren't we the great ones for throwing our rubbish into water?

Cans, bottles, fagends, old mattresses, sewage . . . you name it.

And haven't we been doing it for long enough and to be sparing?

★   ★   ★

"Twenty years ago", wrote John Ruskin in 1866, "there was no lovelier piece of lowland scenery in Southern England . . . than that immediately bordering on the sources of the River Wandel, with all their pools and streams. No clearer or diviner waters ever sang . . ."

But he then went on to describe the "insolent defiling" of those springs by "street and house foulness", the black slime, old metal, and "rags of putrid clothes", the "bricklayer's refuse" and "festering scum" . . . all rotting and stinking "where God meant those waters to bring joy and health".

And he undertook to "cleanse those pools, and trim the flowers about their banks", to purify these "wells of English waters", and restore health and happiness to the heart.

And was regarded as an impractical idealist, even mad.

We could do with such madness today.

So, at your own found spring or well, do what *you* can to honour the spirit of the place. Doesn't have to be much: if there's a can or bottle, fish it out . . . easy as that. Bury any junk in the healing earth, allow the cycle of life and decay to create new life . . . and you'll experience holiness as deeply as in any majestic cathedral.

And if you then wash or even bathe in the purified waters you'll be baptised into the freedom of an elemental happiness which has been waiting to welcome you since the world began.

★   ★   ★

Elemental, because the water of a spring seems changeless, yet always changing, moving in whirls and eddies, flowing to join the "brimming river" on its ways to the seas . . . there to be

79

dragged by the Moon in the great salted tides which surge and ebb, to be drawn up by the heat of the Sun, clouded, driven on the winds . . . to fall as rain, to seep into the earth, to permeate, find a level, trickle . . . become a spring . . .

Whereas trees die – and Sacred Trees and Groves were the other great holy places of those ancient Celts . . . and what can remain? Perhaps some long lingering reputation of the sites where they grew, legends, stories of haunted woods . . . dark forests . . .

Yet, as with their misrepresentations of the attributes and functions of the Great Mother Goddess in the prehistoric world, we have to remember that Jewish and Christian theologians have often behaved more as crude propagandists than scholars in the way they have abused the Sacred Groves. Where they had the temporal power they have ruthlessly destroyed them as "abominations before the Lord" . . . and deliberate suppression of the truth has done the rest.

The depressing fact is that it's not what ever happened in the Sacred Groves that was blasphemous, but what the Children of Jehovah did to the Children of the Great Mother for worshipping Her among the green trees: mass-slaughter of the innocent, even unto ripping the unborn from the living womb . . .

"They shall be burnt with hunger", said their God, "and devoured with burning heat, and with bitter destruction. I will also send the teeth of beasts upon them, with the poison of serpents of the dust. The sword without, and terror within, shall destroy both the young man and the virgin, the suckling also with the man of grey hairs . . . I will make mine arrows drunk with blood, and my sword shall devour flesh, and that with the blood of the slain and of the captives . . . Slay both man and woman, infant and suckling, ox and sheep, camel and ass".

Some of us call that genocide.

*　　*　　*

Robert Graves has probably done more than any merely orthodox scholar to sweeten the air and clear the undergrowth from these tangled places, and allow us to understand the hidden secrets of what the trees meant to our Celtic ancestors . . . and I can only refer you to his book, *The White Goddess*, for an almost literally spell-binding account of the Welsh and Irish Bardic tales, tree-alphabets, and the ivy in its season, and the holly dark green, and the oak and the ash and the Roebuck in the Thicket.

His main idea is that the "language of poetic myth" was a "magical language bound up with ancient religious ceremonies in honour of the Moon Goddess", and that Her function is to remind us of our obligation to "keep in harmony with the family of living creatures" on the one earth we all inhabit . . . because otherwise we will perish before our time. The point being that this "magical language" was an orally transmitted and secret poetic wisdom expressed in knowledge of the names of the trees and their attributes . . . the wisdom concerned with the Seasons, the conflict and reconciliation between the lunar and solar years, and what we need to do in order to achieve that essential harmony between ourselves and our world.

By the present state of our world it's absolutely obvious that we could do worse than listen to any "language" that might help us, whether it comes from the Prophets or the Poets . . . even if they're chanting from the Sacred Groves.

"As the apple tree among the trees of the wood", sings the Rose of Sharon in the *Song of Solomon*, "so is my Beloved among the sons . . . his countenance is like unto the cedars of Lebanon".

Unfortunately, much of our contemporary Folk knowledge about trees is little more than the last vestiges of superstition, almost meaningless at best, at worst sentimental . . . and it most certainly doesn't understand what the Rose of Sharon is actually saying.

The so-called "Christmas" tree is merely the best known example of a Pagan symbol commercially incorporated into a "Christian" festival, while the holly and mistletoe are just as inappropriately grafted onto a religious stock totally at odds and elbows with the Cults of Fertility and the Running Stag of Seven Tines.

Again, we have Yule logs . . . but why? And why is the "fatal yew" a tree of death to be found in churchyards? Why were boys and criminals flogged with *birch*-rods? and Parish boundaries "beaten" with willow-wands or osiers? Why do dowsers use twigs of hazel to trace water? Why does burning elder-wood "summon up" the Devil? Why do children dance around the *mulberry*-bush? Why did a butter-churn usually have a handle of mountain-ash? What was the wood of the maypole? and why is it "unlucky" to bring may-blossom into the house? Who is the Green Man? Why did witches ride on sticks made of broom? Why is the oak the King of the Woods? And why branches of willow in processions on Palm Sunday?

Yes, there *are* serious answers to these questions . . . but most of us no longer even care enough to understand the language of this completely non-technological wisdom. So it's difficult to experience the rich complexity of life "under the greenwood tree" with "no enemy but Winter and rough weather".

Though there are lingering memories, ideas on the shadowed edges of consciousness . . . some trees are decorated annually with garland of flowers or coloured rags, hundreds of people still gather at Glastonbury on Old Christmas Eve to watch the "miraculous" flowering of the Holy Thorn – which was supposed to have sprung from the staff of Joseph of Arimathea, but is merely a winter-flowering hawthorn or applewort, venerated thousands of years before Christ. Again, pilgrims walk to the Major Oak in Sherwood Forest, Oak Apple Day is still just about celebrated, there are Trysting Pines where lovers meet to "plight their troth" by various little ceremonies of holding hands or kissing through convenient holes, we cut hearts and initials in the smooth bark of beech-trees . . . while the phallic worship of the dance around the May-Pole is too obvious to need explaining.

Even William Wordsworth had a pale intimation of what trees can do for those willing to allow for mystery in their days:

"One impulse from a vernal wood
   May teach you more of man,
Or moral evil and of good,
   Than all the sages can".

But, somehow, as with the Holy Wells, these traditions are mostly overlaid with notions about it all being a "harmless bit of fun" or something you do for "Good Luck" . . . or something.

Sanctity, as with so much of our response to the natural world, has become sentimentality.

*   *   *

So make your own way to your nearest good greenwood or dark forest, in bright Spring or golden Autumn . . . it won't be far, not even if measured in miles. And then have eyes to see the sunshine dazzling through the leaves, the dappled shade, the roots fingering into the earth, the trunks rising, the branches reaching . . . have ears for the breathing and rustling of the place, smell the deep damp of last week's rain, feel the "force that through the green fuse drives the flower", the power surging through the blood. And there's that stillness . . .

But are there eyes watching?

Are those movements only birds? rabbits? or *what*?

"Now, who is this? whence came this shrouded majesty?"

How long is time then time has stopped?

And Winter is its own Season, gaunt with storms or stiff with hoar-frost, and you can be alone and lonely, with only the trees for company . . . merely that faint disquiet . . .

Whose eyes "dark as holly"? *Whose* "teeth made of thorns"?

Only the trees, the tall trees, smooth, straight, the shadowy labyrinth of those woods . . . long corridors of arches stretching all ways . . . pointed arches . . .

What cathedral is this?

83

Holy Romans

After the Ages of Bronze and Iron came the Empire of Iron, when the Roman Legions marched across the landscape and "out to Severn strode . . ."

And it's by their straight roads we remember them, so well made that they lasted for centuries after the last Legions had marched back to defend Rome . . . and so well routed that we still follow many of them to this mechanised day. "The old lines remain", wrote John Gloag, "and even when the road has at some time in English history turned aside, a grass-grown lane or a Parish boundary often shows where once the highway ran".

Yet, strangely, not very much else has survived.

True, "Rome only sleeps, she never dies", and her language still lives in the names of so many of our cities and towns: London, from *Londinium* . . . York, from *Eboracum* by way of the Saxon *Eoferwic* and the later *Ebork* . . . every one a page of history. Words, customs, law, civil administration, ways of thinking . . . yes: but there are few remains, few ruins, not many stones by which we could reach and touch them.

Foundations, fallen columns, broken statues, a wall here, some baths there, mosaic pavements, scattered brick villas, occasional shrines to this God or that Goddess . . . places where great Temples once stood . . . a few acres of holy ground where the bones of Rome still rest just under the surface of the landscape.

*   *   *

The most important function of the Roman State Religion was as an "aid to military morale and discipline", rather as with the Church of England during the high days of the British Empire . . . but once the proper pinch of incense had been burned on the altar of the State and Emperor the Roman Authorities were much more tolerant about the various local Gods and Goddesses of their Legions.

This tolerance didn't extend to the Celtic Druids. It's not really certain why, but they probably feared them as a political opposition far more than they objected to their ways of worship. Tacitus, in *The Annals of Imperial Rome*, has a powerfully descriptive passage about their eventual destruction by the Legions under the command of Suetonius.

The attack was in flat-bottomed boats across the shifting shallows of the Menai Strait of Anglesey, where the Druids and Celtic warriors had been driven into their last significant stronghold by previous campaigns.

"The enemy lined the shore in a dense armed mass. Among them were black-robed women with dishevelled hair like Furies, brandishing torches. Close by stood Druids, raising their hands to Heaven and screaming dreadful curses. This weird spectacle awed the Roman soldiers into a sort of paralysis . . . But then they urged each other not to fear a horde of fanatical women. Onward pressed their standards and they bore down their opponents, enveloping them in the flames of their own torches".

And so the Groves were destroyed, the Sacred Trees cut down.

Ah! those long-hafted whetted iron axe-blades!

*   *   *

Anyway, on the evidence of recent excavations, there was a Temple dedicated to the Egyptian Mother Goddess, Isis, in London . . . and at Verulamium, our St Albans, there was an important Shrine to the Roman Mother Goddess, Cybele. And

86

at Colchester there was an enormous Classical Temple dedicated to the Emperor Claudius, so large and magnificent that it rivalled many back in Rome.

*　　*　　*

But, more usually, the foundations and traces which remain are those of small Temples dedicated to the worship of Mithras.

This God of Light was addressed as *Sol invictus*, the Unconquered Sun, and He was depicted as a beautiful young man, lithe strong, and heroic. He was born miraculously from a rock, child of the *Magna Mater*, the Great Mother . . . and He achieved Salvation for humanity by fighting and eventually managing to sacrifice a gigantic bull. It's at this moment of triumph that He's most often represented in statues and paintings: dragging back the head of the rearing bull, cutting its throat, with the streaming blood bringing life to the earth, the corn already sprouting.

For obvious "masculine" reasons His Cult was popular with the Legions, especially on the lonely frontiers of the Empire.

The purpose of His Mysteries was to describe to the initiate the future journey of the soul, with life being seen as a time of "trial" during which the soul is rendered impure. After death the forces of Light and Darkness contend for the soul, and it will be destroyed unless Mithras intervenes . . . so He is the Creative Power of Light, Saviour from Darkness and Death. In fact, the words of a surviving hymn could just as easily be sung in honour of Christ:

"Thou hast saved us by pouring out the Blood Eternal . . ."

No women were allowed to join, there were secret rites of initiation, tests of courage, ordeals by heat and cold, and a final ceremony of acceptance involving baptism by total immersion as a purification – so a ready source of water was necessary to their Temples. They had a Holy Communion of Bread and Water (sometimes mingled with Wine as a symbol of that fruitful Blood), and they worshipped in natural rock caves where they could, or in specially constructed crypts beneath their Temples.

*　　*　　*

There are several bits and pieces in various parts of the country.

One was unearthed about thirty years ago during building excavations in the City of London, close to the Walbrook, a Sacred Stream of the Celts, who threw severed heads and other votive offerings into the water – which means that the place was holy long before the Romans took over the site. Nothing much without the imagination to see: foundations, crumbling walls a foot high, a few square yards of pavement . . . sculpture, coins, bits of broken pottery . . .

It couldn't be preserved where it was found, because an office-block was planned and already being built, and so the whole surviving structure was carefully moved and reassembled on a small area of ground in Queen Victoria Street. And there it is for all who care to look, the crowds passing this way and that on their way to wherever, buses, cars, taxis, lorries, motor-bikes . . . though hardly anybody notices, eyes searching for other things . . . just the occasional American or Japanese tourist, camera focussed.

★   ★   ★

A much more moving Temple of Mithras is up at Carrowburgh in Northumberland, by Hadrian's Wall, not far from that

Sacred Well dedicated to Coventina, the Celtic Fertility Goddess. Remote, lonely, built for the Legions serving out their time on the Wall . . . a few courses of rough stone-work, broken columns, a badly worn carving of the Mother Goddess, irregular pavement slabs, cropped grass, puddles of water . . . the reflected sky . . .

Desecrated by Christians, thrown down, destroyed in the Holy Name of Jesus Christ . . . the Cause of Truth . . .

Yet nothing *but* the Truth is less than the *whole* Truth . . . for that Great Wall once maintained the Roman World, that small rectangular enclosure of hewn stones once held terror and gratitude, sorrow and courage, Mystery and Holy Communion, the Breaking of Bread between Brothers . . . Cleansing by Sanctified Water . . .

How dare we deny holiness to such ground?

Christ at Glastonbury

And then, after the Romans had made the land a colony of the Iron Empire, there came Christ . . .

O pale Galilean . . . hast Thou conquered?

Not yet, not yet – because *this* was when He was a Boy, years before *His* Blood brought another sort of Life to the aching Earth . . . when He came to Glastonbury in Somerset.

★ ★ ★

It all begins with a memory of William Blake's *Jerusalem:*
> "And did those feet in ancient times
> Walk upon England's mountains green?
> And was the holy Lamb of God
> On England's pleasant pastures seen?"

The short answers for some enthusiastic people being "Yes! they *did*" and "He *was!*"

"Blake was a mystic", they say, "knowing the stories associated with Glastonbury and steeped in its ancient history, and he was here clearly quoting the tradition, so dear to every native of the West Country, that Our Lord visited these parts as a Boy or Young Man, and spent some time in quiet retirement here prior to beginning His Ministry in the *other* Holy Land. The words are capable of but one explanation . . . and all such traditions generally spring from a strong foundation of fact".

But before the traditions there are some geographical facts which illuminate them.

In those days of the long ago, what is now the Bristol Channel coast of Somerset, between the Quantocks and the Mendip Hills, was a wide smudge of brackish marshland and sandbanks, with the marshes and shallows extending far inland, over the Bridgwater and Glastonbury Levels, broken here and there by low hummocks of land that rose above sea and mud.

According to Geoffrey Ashe, who has an encylopaedic knowledge of the place and its legends, "much of what seemed like solid ground was morass, fringed by willows and yews, oaks and ash-trees". Glastonbury Tor, the five-hundred-feet high

91

"skewed cone" which dominates the landscape, with its neighbourhood Chalice Hill, was "an island" . . . the enchanted Avalon, Celtic Land of the Dead, where King Arthur was taken by the Four Weeping Queens to be healed of his grievous wounds. And where, during the twelfth century, in a tomb deep beneath the nave of the abbey, his bones were found in a hollowed-out log of oak.

Anyway, this particular tradition of Christ having lived there is garnered from all over Cornwall, Somerset, Gloucestershire, the West of Ireland, and the South of France:

Joseph of Arimathea was a "younger brother of the father of the Virgin Mary", and thus her uncle. He was an "importer in the tin, lead, and copper trade", which then flourished between Cornwall and Phoenicia – the British Isles being known as the *Cassiterides,* or the Islands of Tin . . . which had, in the more distant past, supplied some of the "glorious adornment of Solomon's Temple".

On one of his voyages in a "ship of Tarshish" (modern Cadiz in Spain) he brought the Boy Jesus with him, "who, in exchange for this boyish adventure, revealed certain lost secrets of extracting tin and purging it from its wolfram". They stayed in various parts of Cornwall and Somerset, or "Summer Land" – and, for example, the "little village of Priddy at the top of the Mendip Hills" preserves the "legend that they sojourned there".

Another version has it that "Jesus as a Youth travelled to Britain as a shipwright aboard a trading ship out of Tyre", and was "storm-bound for one winter on the West coast of England".

Fifteen or twenty years later, having "noticed the natural beauty and quiet peace", and "found it to His liking", Jesus returned on His own, and "settled in solemn retirement at Glastonbury". He "built with His own hands a small hermitage of mud and wattle", and "spent some time in quiet study, prayer, and meditation prior to His Ministry and Passion".

There's one possible item of evidence for this, because St Augustine wrote to Pope Gregory the Great about the "first followers of Christ coming to England", and finding a "Church constructed by no human art, but by the Hands of Christ Himself for the Salvation of His people".

Anyway, during this time "He preached here, contacted the Druids, and sowed the seeds of the future Christian Church in our Land". For in "Druid Britain He would be free from the tyranny of Roman oppression, the superstition of Rabbinical misinterpretation, and the grossness of pagan idolatry", and live among a "people dominated by the highest and purest ideals – the very ideals He had come into the world to proclaim".

★   ★   ★

Yes, of course, we are now wandering again in the great Technicolored Kingdom of the imagination . . . and why wouldn't we be?

However, even the most passionately intense of these enthusiasts have to allow that the argument is, at best, "probable", and that the various "authorities" for it are "not conclusive", there being an "absence of clear, reliable, written records". Indeed, the books and pamphlets advocating the legend are loose with "speculations" and such phrases as "may be inferred", "there is the suggestion", "indirect support", "we cannot help feeling", and so on.

They admit that "Joseph of Arimathea's name does not actually appear" in an allegedly "confirmatory" story.

They admit that they have been "unable to elicit the source of an Eastern tradition", though they have "seen it referred to in several cognate works".

They admit that the "claim that Joseph was engaged in the tin trade is only a tradition", even though "fairly widespread".

They admit "we have no conclusive documentary evidence to support these claims".

And, eventually, under the pressure of their own honesty, they are reduced to the "proof" of a positive assertive assumption by the mere absence of its negative: because it is almost impossible to prove "wrong" it must therefore be "right", so *there's* Glory!

There is "no effective argument to the contrary", they say, "and no adequate reason exists why it may not be true".

Then follows the clincher: "One feels in one's heart that it is not possible for it all to be only a beautiful legend without foundation. Why would this story persist through the ages if it were not true?"

And that's their strongest line – the argument from silence: "That Our Lord was absent from Palestine for some time prior to His Ministry finds support in the total lack of any reliable record of His life between the ages of twelve and thirty".

Well, on *those* terms almost anything can be "demonstrated' . . . and off they go in several directions at once.

⋆   ⋆   ⋆

After Joseph of Arimathea had buried "Our Lord in his own rock-tomb, he himself fled from Palestine" at the time of the "persecution which resulted in Stephen's death" . . . and, with eleven disciples, "sought the same place of retreat already hallowed by the residence of Jesus".

They were "received by the local King Aviragis", who "made a grant of land upon them, amounting to twelve hides", one for each member of the group . . . with a "hide" defined as "the area of land which can be cultivated by one man with an ox-drawn plough in a year to support one family", or about one-hundred-and-twenty acres. And these "twelve hides" were recorded in the Domesday Book at the beginning of the eleventh century . . . and are important for some of John Michell's calculations in support of his "squaring of the circle" at Glastonbury.

Anyway, the disciples settled there like the Lord before them, and "Joseph consecrated that little house of mud and wattle as a private chapel". This was later "clad in wood for protection", and became the "first church in Britain", always known as the "Ealde Chiche", or Old Church. In it Joseph "set a wooden likeness he had carved of the Virgin Mary" . . . and a spring "welled from the hillside nearby, and its waters healed the sick".

The "two Holy Cruets containing some of the Blood and Sweat of the Crucified Jesus", which Joseph had brought with him, were "buried in his tomb in the Old Church at Avalon", the romantic name for Glastonbury . . . and the "original Cup of the Last Supper", usually called the "Holy Grail", which he "bought from the innkeeper" whose "Upper Room" it was in which the "First Holy Communion took place", is still "concealed in Chalice Hill where he secretly laid it away against the time of its final triumph".

Incidentally, according to Donald Omand, a Church of England clergyman, an "Exorcist over forty years", Chalice Well has been "repeatedly polluted by visiting Satanists with their unseemly rites", and both he and Dom Robert Petitpierre of Nashdean Abbey have "exorcised it at separate times" – on each of which the "healing was only temporary". Which at least suggests that the place obviously retains *some* sort of power – for those who come in seriousness, whether good or evil, or even merely curious, must be drawn by "matters beyond the normal".

There *are* those who believe that this particular Holy Grail actually exists, though no longer "concealed in Chalice Hill" . . . and several claimants to be the "genuine original" have been proffered, all the subject of considerable controversy and conflicting pamphlets.

One of these Holy Cups, which "legend associates" with

Glastonbury, is owned by a married couple in Hereford. It's made of olive-wood, "small, gnarled, darkened with age", and "two-thirds is missing", the "remainder split and joined together with two copper rivets". It must have been "about three inches deep, with no decoration except a faint scoring of three bands on the outside".

The story is both interesting and typical of these legends: "Revered as a priceless relic of Christ it was kept at Glastonbury Abbey" until Henry the Eighth began looting the monasteries during the Protestant Reformation, when it was "taken by seven monks for safe keeping to an abbey in Wales". But then Thomas Cromwell "descended on that place", and the "Holy Cup was eventually entrusted by the last of the monks" to a "devout family" until "such time as the Church should claim it back". And so it has "come down" to this couple . . . who've "insured it for a thousand pounds".

As though anybody could doubt, it has "healing properties", and "many people have drunk water out of it" and been "cured". Requests from "Wales and all over the world" used to arrive for "water out of the Holy Cup", and until very recently the present owners would "send out little plastic bottles of water that had been in a glass bowl with the Grail". After a "remarkable local cure" they were "deluged with appeals", as many as "fifteen hundred in one week". There was "no charge" for this service, though "sometimes people would send some money or a postal order to cover the costs of postage". However, the "majority didn't", and the expense was such that now the "Holy Grail has been taken into hiding". And, for many years, there has been a "petition" asking for the "return of the Holy Grail" to its "rightful place".

*　　*　　*

But that is by no means all of the Christian legends of Glastonbury.

For the Virgin Mary also came to this country to escape Roman and Jewish persecution, and lived in "Our Lady's Dowry", being that "self-same little wattle temple built with His own hands by the Lord at Avalon". She "finished Her earthly travail in Britain", and was "laid to rest here in AD48".

True, the Roman Catholic Church believes that She was "assumed bodily into Heaven", but this Blessed Assumption *could* have been from Glastonbury as easily as from anywhere else, surely.

Mary Magdalene and the "Two Sisters of Bethany" lived with the Virgin Mary, and "the Magdalene's classic beauty and rich voice endeared her so deeply to the hearts of the people that she was adored as a saint before she died". And even the main road through today is Magdalene Street.

Simon Zelotes "evangelised" in Britain, and died a "martyr's death by crucifixion at Caistor, Lincolnshire, on 10th. May, AD61".

Lazarus, the "man whom Jesus had raised from the dead", though "his stay was but short", left his "timeless imprint" on the country.

Mary Salome and Mary Cleophas, "two of those who witnessed the death of Christ on the Cross", lived here with a "Negro servant girl, Sara". . . who subsequently became the Patron Saint of thieves and gypsies.

And to this "hallowed haven many of Our Lord's original Disciples came – James the Just, Brother of Jesus, and Barnabas, Zaccheus, and Luke". Finally, the "bodies of Peter and Paul", with the "remains of the martyrs Lawrence, Gregory, and Pancras", are "buried in England . . . the most hallowed ground on earth".

Which should make Glastonbury holy enough for anybody, surely?

*   *   *

Little or nothing survives: the ruins of the abbey church built in the thirteenth century on the traditional site of that wattle hut, the legends, dreams, books and pamphlets in the gift-shops . . . words . . .

And yet I'd rather live in that landscape of the mind than in the concrete world we have made from our gentle yearnings.

No, legends are not "records of facts" . . . but the *need* for such legends is a fact more important than any such records.

*   *   *

97

There's a final "prophecy" uttered in "oracular Latin" by Melkin, a fifth-century Celtic Bard: "Joseph hath with him in his tomb two cruets, white and silver, one filled with the Blood and the other with the Sweat of Jesus. When the tomb shall be found entire, intact, in time to come, it shall be seen and shall be open unto all the world. Thenceforth nor water nor the dew of Heaven shall fail the dwellers in that Ancient Isle . . ."

The Early English Church

After the legends of Glastonbury, which still sound out like great bronze gongs across the landscape, the first authentic record of Christianity in this country is that of the Venerable Bede, writing at the beginning of the eighth century.

"In the one-hundred-and-fifty-sixth year after Our Lord's Incarnation", he says in *A History of the English Church and People*, "while the holy Eleutherus ruled the Roman Church as Pope, Lucius, a British King, sent him a letter, asking to become a Christian under his instruction. This pious request was immediately granted, and the Britons received the Faith . . ."

True, Lucius is now regarded as an apocryphal king, but it's a pity to spoil a good story for a pennorth of petty fact.

Anyway, the word of the King was obviously law in those day, because the "Britons held to the Faith peacefully in all its purity and fullness" until the persecutions fifty or so years later . . . which resulted in the first authentic English martyr, St Alban.

*   *   *

He was, according the Bede, a citizen of the important chartered Roman city of Verulamium when the "unbelieving Emperors were issuing savage edicts against all Christians". Though "as yet a Pagan", he sheltered a fugitive priest, was converted by "this man's unbroken activity of prayer and vigil", and began to follow his "example of faith and devotion". Other sources say that Alban was actually a "Roman soldier", and name the priest as Amphibalus.

When the legionaries arrived to search the house, Alban "at once surrendered himself in the place of his guest and teacher", and was "led bound before the Tribunal". After cross-examination, in which he "declared himself a Christian" and refused to burn incense on the altars of Jupiter and Apollo, his old Gods, he was "flogged by the executioners", but "bore the most horrible torments patiently and even gladly". The "infuriated" Tribunal then "ordered his immediate decapitation".

When the mandatory miracles started.

He was "led out to execution", but the squad of escorting legionaries came to the "River Ver which flowed swiftly between the wall of the city and the place appointed" . . . and they couldn't get over the bridge because of the "great crowd of men and women of all ages and conditions, who were moved by God's will to attend the death of this holy man". So Alban, "who ardently desired a speedy martyrdom, approached the river", and, "as he raised his eyes to Heaven in prayer", the "river ran dry in its bed" and "left them a way to cross".

When the executioner saw this he was "so moved in spirit" that he "threw down his drawn sword", and "begged that he might be thought worthy to die with Alban if he could not die in his place". Naturally enough, the "other executioners hesitated to pick up the sword from the ground".

Alban then "ascended a small hill", neither "crag nor cliff", but a "gently rising slope made smooth by nature", a "lovely spot as befitted the occasion, clad in a happy mantle of many kinds of flowers". As he "reached the summit, holy Alban asked God to give him water", and at once a "perpetual spring bubbled up at his feet".

Here, then, he "met his death", and "reached the crown of life which God has promised to those who love Him".

But the man "whose impious hands struck off that pious head was not permitted to boast of his deed, for as the martyr's head fell, the executioner's eyes dropped out on the ground".

And then a "beautiful church worthy of this martyrdom was built", says Bede, "where sick folk are healed and frequent miracles take place to this day".

Which is all innocently typical of the way in which these legends grow, with almost every element from instantaneous conversion and miraculous wells to severed heads and immediate Divine vengance on the unrepentant.

★   ★   ★

Six hundred years later, at the end of the eighth century, the long-lost hiding-place of St Alban's head and body was "miraculously revealed" in a dream to Offa, King of Mercia, who then established and richly endowed a Benedictine Abbey to replace the small wooden church on the site of the martyrdom . . . and the first Norman Abbot after the Conquest, Paul of Caen, had a larger one built there in the eleventh century, using Roman bricks from the ruins of Verulamium – and this is still the central part of today's cathedral: with both cathedral and city named St Albans.

There are all the usual grey facts and dreary figures: the cathedral "stands on higher ground (three-hundred-and-twenty feet) than any other in England" . . . the "Nave (at two-hundred-and-seventy-five feet) is the longest Medieval example after Winchester in existence" . . . a "new Chapter House, which provided a Refectory and a Gift-Shop, was recently opened by Her Majesty the Queen . . ."

But at the heart of the place, behind the High Altar, was the elaborately carved marble Shrine of the Saint – which, inevitably, was smashed and almost destroyed during the Protestant Reformation . . .

Listen! you can hear those unholy hammers, still see those same unforgiving faces on the streets, know that it would all be done again today if the orders were given. Always men willing to obey orders.

Weren't the great churches of Coventry and London and Berlin and Dresden destroyed during the Second World War? Do you remember the old Benedictine Monastery of Monte Casino? Even the small domestic altars of Hiroshima and Nagasaki?

However, what can be smashed can sometimes be restored, and, late in the nineteenth century, that elaborately carved marble Shrine was painstakingly reconstructed from more than two thousand collected and hoarded fragments. Angels, arches, iron grilles, leaves, flowers, the stone worn and ravaged, hallowed . . .

*   *   *

Yet there aren't any bones, nor *have* there been . . . for how long?

Since, at the very latest, that day when the Shrine was desecrated by Thomas Cromwell's men: say four hundred years . . . and what *they* did with the bones isn't known for sure.

Even *those* bones could hardly have been the genuine remains of St Alban, because the original Saxon Monastery was sacked by the Danes around 870, about a hundred years after it was built, and these raiders carried them off to Odense in Denmark, where they were deposited in a Benedictine Monastery. True, there's a more complicated version of the legend, involving a specially prepared set of fake bones being sent to the monks at Ely in order to mislead the Danes, and the monks at Ely keeping *them* as genuine and sending yet *another* fake set back to the monks at St Albans . . . and an even less likely variant about a monk of St Albans going to that Benedictine Monastery at Odense, posing as a postulant, eventually being made Sacristan – when he stole back the bones, and thus restored them to their proper Shrine.

But, whichever of these various sets of fake or genuine bones were those originally enshrined in that Saxon Monastery, it's highly improbable that St Albans head or body or bones could have been preserved for the six hundred years between his death and their "miraculous" discovery by King Offa. Yes, they might *just* have been genuine . . . but the manufacture and trade in such relics was a thriving industry in the Dark and Middle Ages, and this particular set of bones has all the marks of both pious and commercial invention.

*   *   *

Remember Chaucer's Pardoner? *He* had a "rubble of pig's bones" to astound country parsons and congregations.

Because manufacture and trade it most certainly was.

For one wicked example, at the beginning of the thirteenth century the Cistercian Abbey of Hailes, in Gloucestershire, bought a crystal phial of the Holy Blood of Christ, which carried with it a certificate of authentication signed by the Patriarch of Jerusalem, who later became Pope Urban the Fourth.

Not surprisingly, the Abbey soon became one of the most renowned centres of pilgrimage in the whole country, and tens of thousands of good people would come to venerate this precious relic of their Salvation.

In the fourteenth century the Pardoner would take his oath on it:

"By Goddes precious herte, and by his nailes,
And by the Blood of Christ that is in Hailes".

Margery Kempe, the Mystic of King's Lynn, went to see it in the fifteenth century, and "was shriven and had loud cries and boisterous weepings".

And in the sixteenth century it was even more popular: "You would wonder to see how they come by flocks out of the West Country to many images", wrote Hugh Latimer, who was then the Vicar of a church on one of the many roads to the Abbey. "But chiefly to the Blood of Hailes".

Well, Latimer, Bishop of Worcester, was eventually burnt alive at the stake by the orders of Mary Tudor for his Protestant Faith . . . but he was right about that "Holy Blood" if nothing else. Because when it was removed by Thomas Cromwell's men it was found to be "clarified honey coloured with saffron".

And there were vast stores of these fraudulent "relics" all over Britain and Europe: many more phials and clots and smears of Holy Blood, Holy Shrouds, beams and pieces and splinters of the True Cross, hundreds of Holy Nails, several complete Crowns of Thorns and dozens of twigs, racks of Holy Spears, thongs from the Holy Scourge, six or seven Seamless Robes, crumbs from the Holy Bread of the Last Supper, crusts from the Five Miraculous Loaves, drops of Holy Wine . . . hairs from the Holy Head, slivers of Holy Fingernails, other phials of Holy Sweat or Holy Tears, five or six claimants for the Holy Navel . . . pints of the Virgin Mary's Milk, wardrobes of Her Holy Clothes and Girdles (the Pardoner had "Our Lady's Veil" in his box), stools on which She was sitting at the Annunciation, pillows She used, towels, sandals, wedding-rings . . . even a proliferation of Holy Foreskins, the actual flesh of Jesus the Incarnate God: with twelve or thirteen of *these* still being venerated to this day in various churches of Italy and Spain.

Probably the most outrageous of them all, at least in England, was the famous Rood at the Cistercian Monastery of Boxley in Kent, which pilgrims were encouraged to visit on their way to the Shrine of St Thomas at Canterbury. This was a "miraculous" crucifix on which the figure of Christ "rolled its eyes, opened its mouth, moved its head, and rotated its hands in a gesture of blessing" as an answer to the prayers offered before it". When Thomas Cromwell's men came in the sixteenth century the wires which "worked" it from the back were exposed, and the cruel fraud was destroyed.

And even my own little village church at Trimingham, miles from nearly everywhere in Remote Norfolk, was once supposed to have the "head of St John the Baptist" . . . an honour it shared with dozens of other places which couldn't afford to buy anything more closely associated with Christ.

Does any of it really matter?

Well, there's little to be said in defence of the fakers and con-men and conspiring monks, all those who have over the centuries knowingly lied to and exploited the credulous or innocent: the Christian Church has a lot to answer for.

But to believe is its own reward, the pleasures of faith are without price . . . and so the Shrine of St Alban and all other such holy places are more or less what *you* make them.

Don't be too disappointed at what you find there: all too often you'll merely see a notice on the wall near where a martyrdom occured or a saint died, or there'll be a yard or so of pavement roped-off, or a few weathered stones in the grass . . . but you are reminded that these people were, as G. M. Trevelyan put it, "men and women who lived and breathed like us, and are now gone, like ghosts at cockcrow".

Know the truth, yes.

Understand the deceptions and priestly evasions and disingenuous bits of less-than-the-truth, yes.

But don't allow any mere faker or priest to rob you of your heritage.

Those men and women like us have lived and died for what they believed, been tortured and martyred for their faith. You don't even have to agree with what they believed, you can utterly reject their faith . . . and yet you can retain the capacity to be moved by their sacrifice, to feel a better and happier person for having known about them.

St Alban and so many of the others may even be figments of legend in their totality, creatures of some collective dream . . . but they can still "move and have their being" in your imagination, speak while you listen, weep and laugh with you, and release you with blessings into the landscape of love and joy and peace.

Through the Mists of Avalon

Whether or not Jesus Christ ever actually came to Glastonbury, there's little doubt that a church of some sort was built on the traditional site of that "small hermitage of mud and wattle" quite early in the history of English Christianity.

For when, at that request of the apocryphal King Lucius mentioned by Bede, two missionaries arrived from Rome at the end of the second century, they "found an old church built, as it was said by the hands of Christ's disciples . . . which church the Heavenly Builder Himself showed to be consecrated by many miraculous deeds . . . with the whole story in ancient writings . . ."

And when the invading Saxons reached the place in the middle of the seventh century they found an already old Chapel "reinforced by planks and strips of lead". It was about sixty feet long, nearly thirty feet across, had three small windows in one side and a larger one at the end . . . and was in the care of a monastery with many Irish monks.

Even the late Professor Trehane, who was a learned critic of the Glastonbury legends, had to admit that the Saxons "found a great and famous Celtic monastery already established and flourishing there, already venerated as the holiest place in Britain".

And this "Ealde Chiche" was still in existence when William of Malmesbury wrote his *Antiquities of Glastonbury Church* in the early twelfth century. It was eventually dignified with the Latin of *Vetusta Ecclesia*, and larger and larger structures were built around it.

The first of which there's any trace was ordered by Ine, King of the West Saxons, at the beginning of the eighth century . . . who also "refurbished the monastery" and "enriched it with gifts".

It became an Abbey of the Benedictine Rule in the middle of the tenth century, and, under St Dunstan as Abbot, it grew famous as an important centre of piety and learning.

St Dunstan later became Archbishop of Canterbury, and when he died there was an "unedifying dispute" between the monks of Canterbury and those of Glastonbury as to the "whereabouts" of his "genuine" bones . . . with the Pope eventually "rebuking" the new Abbott of Glastonbury for his "blatant dishonesty" about a fake set.

Anyway, the first Norman Abbot after the Conquest added various bits and pieces. It had always been a place of pilgrimage, but now it expanded and found wider and wider fame. There was a "great treasury of relics", many hostels for pilgrims, and the town prospered.

Then, at the end of the twelfth century, most of the abbey, including the *Vetusta Ecclesia,* was burnt to the foundations. Rebuilding started at once, with the Lady Chapel first, "on the site of the old wooden church" and "in strict fidelity to the ancient plan". And the greater part of the vast new building was finished in about a hundred years.

It's the ruin of this Abbey you can see today: suppressed and looted by Thomas Cromwell's men in the sixteenth century, the stained-glass smashed, the lead of the roof torn off and "melted by burning the carved woodwork" . . . neglected for three hundred years, the Lady Chapel blown apart by the bomb of a Protestant enthusiast in the early eighteenth century, the whole place used as a free quarry by local people . . . with one final irony being that the Abbot's Kitchen escaped most of this vandalism by being rented to the Quakers for a Meeting House. Eventually, at the beginning of this century, the site was acquired on the quiet by the Church of England.

A few piers of stone, walls, arches, foundations, floor tiles, bits of pavement . . . turnstiles, charges for admission . . . gift-shop . . .

*　　*　　*

But there, before where the High Altar used to stand, neat and tidy in the turf, is the slab marking the tomb of King Arthur and his Queen, the "most beautous and gentle Lady", Guinevere.

And another dimension opens, legend merges with legend: Joseph of Arimathea brings the Holy Grail to Glastonbury, and buries it in Chalice Hill . . . and here is King Arthur, seeker for that Mystic Holy Grail, buried within sight of that same Chalice Hill.

"King Arthur", say Janet and Colin Bord, "is both man and myth, but where one ends and the other begins it is almost impossible to judge".

The man was probably Artorius, a chieftain of the fifth century, who led British warriors in a victorious campaign against the invading Saxons: a foot-note in the history books . . . but the myth of Camelot and the Round Table and the Holy Grail lives and thrives to this day.

Tintagel, Uther Pendragon, Merlin, Excalibur, Guinevere, Lancelot, Morgan le Fay, the Last Battle, Mordred, the Dolorous Stroke, the Mortal Wound, the Four Weeping Queens, the Isle of Avalon . . . all these are as the sound of the high silver trumpets . . . now to join another music.

"Where falls not hail, or rain, or any snow . . ."

★   ★   ★

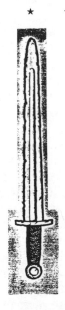

It seems that after the disastrous fire at the end of the twelfth century, when the Norman Abbey was almost totally destroyed, the monks "rediscovered" King Arthur's burial place. True, there were ancient sources which said that he "slept in the lost and legendary Land of Lyonesse", or on an "enchanted isle" off the West Coast or Ireland . . . but a Welsh Bardic tradition

109

claimed that he was "buried between two pillars in Glastonbury Abbey". And there *were* two such pillars: as described by William of Malmesbury, they were probably the broken shafts of Saxon crosses. Well, as the monks "levelled the ground" for the new Abbey, "seven feet down between the pillars" they unearthed a "broad slab of stone" . . . though, unless they were actually digging to find the grave, it's uncertain what they were doing that deep.

Which is the first indication that the "discovery" might not have been quite so innocent as it's meant to sound.

An "eye-witness" continues the tale: "On that syde" of the slab "that layed downwards was found a thin plate of lead in the form of a cross, and on that syde of the plate towards the stone was engraven in rude and barbarous characters this inscription, HIC JACET SEPULTUS INCLYTUS REX ARTURUS IN INSULA AVALLONIA".

Here lies buried King Arthur in the Isle of Avalon.

As late as two-hundred-and-fifty years afterwards John Leland, the historian, wrote that he'd seen this "cross of lead" and "held it in his hand" . . . it's known to have survived to the seventeenth century, because William Camden published an engraved drawing of it in 1607 . . . there's a mention of it a hundred years after that . . . and some True Believers think it could well be "lost" in an attic or drawer somewhere to this day.

Anyway, "nine feet" below the slab was the "great trunk of a tree", a "hollowed oaken log", probably a dug-out boat, which was apparently embedded in the ground at a slight angle . . . an interesting detail, as this was how the Celts would place the coffins of their great warriors: a fact the monks could hardly have invented if they were faking.

Inside this ritually significant "oaken log" were his bones, "of large size", and his "skull was perceived to bear ten wounds, one of which was very grievous".

The Queen's bones were next to his, "slighter, perfect and whole, and her hair was found to be neatly plaited, and of the colour of burnished gold" . . . which "being touched by the fingers of one who watched, it fell into dust under his hand".

And into ashes all her dreams . . .

These two sets of bones were "stored in a pair of painted wooden chests" . . . and, eventually, towards the end of the thirteenth century, they were "enwrapped in precious cloths, replaced in their chests", and buried before the High Altar at the place still marked by that Official slab and accompanying notice.

★   ★   ★

Now, as many realists have pointed out, the monks badly needed funds for the rebuilding of the Abbey . . . so, according to Warwick Rodwell, they "duly dug in their cemetery and produced bones which they announced to the world as the remains of King Arthur and Guinevere". The implication being that they also faked that cross of lead – though that would have been well within their competence and scope.

Genuine or not, it all worked, because "in consequence pilgrims virtually deserted the cathedral at Wells" a few miles away, and "flocked instead to Glastonbury".

Again, it's been suggested that there were "political reasons" for the "discovery" at that particular time. According to William Purcell, it was Henry the Second who "encouraged the search for the grave" as he was having trouble with an "unquiet Wales", where the belief was that an "heroic King, Arthur of memory, would one day awake from his sleep in Avalon to lead them to victory" against the hated English. And a dead King Arthur, with bones to prove his death, would at least discourage such thoughts of glory.

But whether the reasons for the digging were political or monkish, innocent or devious, the legend has lasted ever since.

And by now King Arthur is the personification of Chivalry, Defender of the Faith against the Forces of Darkness, and a symbol of our natural yearning for the "establishment of earthly rule on a basis of justice and compassion".

Not everybody sees it in those Technicolored terms: "When I first went to Arthur's Grave", wrote Fay Weldon, the novelist, who has lived in Glastonbury, "I saw it as nothing but a tourist trap. But then I went again one evening, and it *was* nuministic – it was transmitting – there was this odd still feeling of something going on. A brooding power, not evil in itself, but indifferent, and certainly unhelpful".

But most people who believe at all are *believers*, sold and

111

singing.

So all of that is the other dimension to Glastonbury: the tracing of those ideals through the mists of Avalon, their complex merging with the legends of Christ walking in "England's green and pleasant land" . . . that "Countenance Divine" shining forth "upon our clouded hills" . . . the hope of a New Jerusalem which will one day be built here.

O clouds, unfold!

             ★   ★   ★

But even *that* is not all there is to the place . . . because beneath the petrol-pumps and supermarkets of the streets, behind the gift-shops and guide-books, beyond what you can see of the Abbey and the Tor and the tatty souvenirs, there's yet another realm.

As with Stonehenge, and so many other equally mysterious places, there's that Sacred Geometry, the Squaring of the Circle . . . a different order of reality . . . and John Michell is its Prophet.

The argument is complicated, difficult, diffuse, and sometimes even fanciful . . . but, briefly, he has rediscovered what he believes to be the "metaphysical foundations" that "enabled the geomancers of old to build Glastonbury Abbey to the precise dimensions" which would "cause the structure to become a Temple for the interaction of terrestrial and solar energies". It all involves the ancient links between language and arithmetic, words and numbers, interlocking circles as symbols of Heaven and Hell with the Earth between, Spirit and Matter, soul and body . . . and much, much more besides.

             ★   ★   ★

That nothing ought to be accepted as true which "can not be proved so in two ways", by "reason and poetic intuition".

That Christ, born at the beginning of the Ages of Pisces, the Zodiacal Sign of the Fish, was "Ikthus the Fish, the letters of which name form the initials of the Greek phrase Jesus Christ, Son of God, Savior".

That the *vesica piscis*, the geometrical Sign of the Fish,

formed by those interlocking circles, was "adopted as the basic figure of Christian architecture and iconography", an obvious example being the "Mandorla that surrounds representations of Christ in Glory" . . . as in the Graham Sutherland tapestry behind the High Altar of Coventry cathedral.

That the image of the "Temple of Jerusalem restored" has become accepted in the language of symbolism as "representing the eternal aspiration of Mystics" to witness the "appearance of a revealed world order, necessary for the re-estiblishment of a truly human civilisation".

That, after the destruction of the actual Temple of Jerusalem, the "symbolic Temple" of the New Jerusalem in the Book of Revelation was accepted by the early Christians as a structure by means of which they could "perceive, however fleetingly, the architecture of Creation", and "gain some insight" into the "ancient dream of the Divine Order of Heaven translated to Earth".

That those interlocking circles are the Keys into this lost Kingdom of Wisdom.

And that they are drawn in the Landscape of Glastonbury . . . which is thus, for those with eyes to see, the English Jerusalem.

*   *   *

Because do you remember those "twelve hides of land" granted by King Aviragus to Joseph of Arimathea and the eleven disciples?

Well, one hide was one-hundred-and-twenty acres. So twelve hides would be one-thousand-four-hundred-and-forty acres . . . which has the same "numerical proportions" as the New Jerusalem described and "measured in such precise detail" by St John in the Book of Revelation: making Glastonbury a "microcosm of that Cosmic Temple".

The scale varies, the numbers remain mysteriously constant.

And there's all manner of more or less convincing evidence that Glastonbury, like many other sacred buildings, was indeed laid out on some curious ground-plan involving interlocking circles and Pythagorean triangles . . . and that the builders "made it plain for those with eyes to see" what was going on.

"In the pavement of the Old Church", wrote our friend,

113

William of Malmesbury, an Anglo-Norman priest in the twelfth century, "may be remarked on every side stones designedly interlaid in triangles and squares, and sealed" (these days we'd say ornamented or outlined) "with lead, in which I believe some *arcanum sacrum* is contained . . ."

Some Sacred Mystery . . .

It was all a common enough idea in the Middle Ages: indeed, Dante ends *The Divine Comedy* with a Vision of God as the Light Eternal at the heart of "three great circles of three colours", two "reflecting each other" as "rainbow by rainbow", and the third "as it were fire". "Like the geometer who sets his mind to the squaring of the circle", he says, "and does not discover the principle he needs, such was I at the sight. I desired to see how the image was fitted to the circle, and how it has its place there . . ."

But he can't, his "powers fail the High Phantasy" . . . and the Poem ends with the sudden flash of Mystical Illumination that it's "Love which moves the Sun and all the other Stars".

His point is that just as a circle is immeasurable in terms of a square, so the Divine is inexpressible in terms of humanity.

Again, there was a famous clock in Glastonbury Abbey, looted or destroyed during the Protestant Reformation, made in the fourteenth century by an artist-craftsman of the Community, Peter Lightfoot. He made several such remarkable instruments, one of which survives to this day in full working-order at Wells cathedral. By contemporary accounts they were similar in size and design.

A dial-plate over six feet in diameter, "contained in a square frame like the plan of the New Jerusalem, in the corners of which are Angels holding the Four Winds". The outer circle is divided into "twenty-four hours of the day", and a "large gilt Sun" points to the hour as it "moves round the Earth". An "inner circle shows the minutes", a "small star moves round the circle every hour", and a "third circle gives the days of the Lunar Month" . . . while a "Crescent with a pointer shows the age of the Moon . . ."

Yes, there are those Squared Circles, the microcosm and macrocosm, humanity as the image of the Universe . . . time as a function of the Cosmic Temple . . .

Agreed, it probably sounds faintly dotty, even demented: but it's at the very least as fascinating as a good crossword-puzzle . . . and the ultimate solution is undoubtedly more satisfying.

"Yet", writes John Michell, "few people have the time or inclination to examine evidence which might disturb the settled convictions to which they have grown accustomed".

But that's exactly what you have to do before you can dismiss it all as codswallop: "Examine evidence", read his books, allow him to "disturb" your perhaps "settled convictions" . . . visit Glastonbury with a mind open to these ideas, receptive to the spirit and atmosphere of the place, wander around, have a look at this and that, listen to the ancient voices, the silent music . . . climb to the top of the Tor, breathe that air, see the secret landscape shimmering above and below the twentieth century . . .

And do all this *before* you deny that John Michell may be aware of certain "cloud-capped towers", distant glimpses of the New Jerusalem, prophetic visions . . .

Because to neglect these mysteries in favour of our present technological obessions is to ask for trouble . . . and wouldn't you agree that we're already in trouble? *deep* trouble?

From the "rational" point of view there's no reason to doubt that "within the next few years" the earth will be destroyed by war, the wastes of nuclear energy generation, or environmental pollution, and that humanity will die out. The fertility of the soil and our limited stock of mineral resources are already threatened, and "further exploitation will shortly put an end to both".

And ancient wisdom suggests that to change the world you must first change your country, to change your country you must first change your city, to change your city you must first change your family, and to change your family you must first change yourself . . . and where better to see a way of possible change than in these twelve hides of holy ground?

"Everything possible to be believed", wrote William Blake, "is an image of the truth".
And the truth will make us free.

★　　★　　★

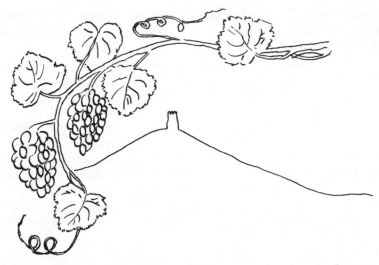

Mind you, even with all that said, there *are* dangers . . . because the whole idea of Secret Wisdom implies that it's *knowledge* which will save us – whereas we need love, emotions, feelings, the experience of life rather than more and more information about less and less important technologies.

We want secrets rather less than simple human goodness, for it's not what we *know* that matters, but what we *are*: not that we believe in so many words and creeds and declarations, but what we do.

Again, as Geoffrey Ashe points out, "Secret Wisdom involves a good deal of unhealthy spell-weaving, numerology, and the conjuration of spirits . . ."

All you have to do to be warned is walk down Fisher Hill into Glastonbury on any moderately busy Summer afternoon, on along Magdalene Street, turn right up the High Street as far as the church of St John the Baptist, cross to the other pavement, and then walk back past the tea-rooms the way you've come . . . and look in the gift-shops at the books and pamphlets and souveniers and trinkets, watch the crowds . . .

Because some, *some* of the junk you will see is commercial exploitation of the genuinely spiritual quite as wicked as that of many cathedral towns, and *some* of the people are obviously performing for all the world to stare. "As a place attracting cranks and gurus and visionaries", says Geoffrey Ashe, "as well

116

as seekers of a saner and wiser kind, Glastonbury is the Los Angeles of England".

Walk your *own* way, then, do your own thing: innocence is its own and best defence. The Divine *is* there to be experienced.

★　　★　　★

There are several more mysteries worth your wonder.

One is that the whole landscape is a Temple of the Stars.

"The Glastonbury Giants", says Mary Caine, an informed enthusiast, "lie sleeping around a vast circle in the hallowed Vale of Avalon . . . the largest, the oldest, the most enigmatic of all the antiquities of Britain. They are too good to be true, and too big to be seen – and what can't be seen can't be believed, at least in our day and age".

The claim is that "with large-scale maps and aerial photography" it is possible to "trace the outlines of huge symbolic figures" around the place. They are inside a circle ten miles across, are "delineated by streams and old roadways and boundaries of ancient fields", represent the Signs of the Zodiac, and are "related to incidents in the cycle of the Holy Grail".

For the Zodiac is apparently a "cryptogram containing in economical picture-form the teaching underlying all Ancient Religions", the very "fountain-head of all Myth", and the "secret source of all the various legends of Avalon".

And there you go: because, as well as the familiar Signs from Aquarius to Pisces, with, mysteriously, Virgo hugely pregnant, 'Arthur, Guinevere, Merlin, and all the chief Knights of the Holy Grail, are still stitting at this Round Table!"

According to Geoffrey Ashe, it's also been suggested that "there was once a canopy of ice crystals in the upper atmosphere" which reflected the figures "for the benefit of those below".

Yes, some of these outlines are obviously *there* . . . but others "demand the eye of faith". Like the "ink-blot test" or "seeing pictures in the fire", you probably get out what you put in.

And where is it written that *thou shalt not dream dreams?*

★　　★　　★

117

Another mystery is that expounded by Geoffrey Ashe himself: that Glastonbury Tor, which is a "natural hill", has "also been artificially shaped", with the "still visible terraces around it" being the "principal remains of a maze" . . . a "long, twisting, devious, ritual spiral", which winds "seven times around to the summit". He calls it the "Cretan Spiral", because it "appears on Cretan coins", and has "some connexion with the legend of the Labyrinth".

What was it for?

Remember those Celtic spirals at New Grange? and them being symbols of death and rebirth? with the Winter of Death known as Spiral Castle?

Well, that's one element: the ritual tracing of the spiral as a reminder of the great cycle . . . circling into the maze and out again seen as the turning of the season, "into the darkness and constriction of Winter, and out again into the light and liberation of Spring" . . . symbolic experiences to reinforce spiritual beliefs.

Another element is that the "Glastonbury hill-profile evokes a recumbent female figure, with the Tor forming the left breast, Chalice Hill a pregnant belly". Which suggests that the Great Goddess or Earth Mother is also present there, especially as "early images" of Her "do occasionally have lines circling and meandering on their bodies". As in Crete, She was "Mistress of the Labyrinth", and "inside Her was the Underworld", the Tomb as well as Womb.

Again, threading the maze may have been a ceremonial re-enactment of the Quest for the Holy Grail . . . with yet another theme being that of the "ascent of the Holy Mountain", thus linking Glastonbury with Dante's *Divine Comedy* in one more way: for the Mount of Purgatory has seven ascending cornices or tiers . . . the Seven-Storey Mountain being a powerful image in the Middle Ages, the basis of many Mystical ideas about the journey of the soul up to God.

"The facts and possibilities do exist", says Geoffrey Ashe. "Combined, they support the belief that Glastonbury is rooted in very ancient realities".

And you can't be saying much fairer than that, now can you?

★   ★   ★

The last surviving monk of Glastonbury Abbey, Austin Ringwode, lived "in prayer and fasting and vigil" until 1587, and on his death-bed he is supposed to have uttered this prophecy:

"The Abbey will one day be repaired and rebuilt for the like worship which has ceased, and then peace and plenty will for a long time abound".

Sleep, Brother Ringwode . . . sleep . . .

The Early Saints

Well now, St Patrick may not have been the first of our British Saints, but wasn't he the brightest and best, surely? And wouldn't any half-way decent Irish scholar and gentleman fight you for daring to be saying otherwise?

"They would take up arms to fight the waves of the sea", Aristotle is supposed to have said ... though when did *he* ever have the pleasure of meeting the likes of St Patrick?

Anyway, we've already traipsed from Wicklow to Tara of the High Kings after Himself, and from there westward to Mag Slecht and Crom Cruach and the Mountain of Croagh ... so let's be considering some others of those early Saints of God.

*   *   *

Mind you, though the Celtic Church flourished and that "Ealde Chiche" was watched over by the Irish monks at Glastonbury, the Anglo-Saxons would at first have nothing of Christianity, preferring their own Dark Gods ... their names still living among us, full of blood and their own truth ...

Monandaeg, the day sacred to the Moon.

Tiwes daeg, the day sacred to Tiw, God of War.

Wodnes daeg, the day sacred to Woden, or Wotan, King of the Gods, Master of Fury, Leader of the Wild Hunt – also known as Odin.

Thures daeg, the day sacred to Thor, Son of Woden, God of Thunder, armed with the Hammer.

Frigedaeg, the day sacred to Frigga, wife to Woden, Goddess of the Sky, Queen of Heaven, having dominion over the Abode of the Dead ...

Yes, we remember them, those Gods of war and battles and feastings, their swords of iron clank and clash through the stony places, their fires ring our Northern hills, and our forests are often strangely silent at their unbidden presence ... and from the departure of the Roman Legions at the beginning of the fifth century, until the arrival of St Augustine on the coasts of Kent at the end of the sixth, these terrible Strangers ruled more than the days of the week.

But then came St Augustine to "recover" the country for Christianity, landing at Thanet with his companions, who are said to have been "forty in number", where they were visited by King Ethelbert, and "granted a freedom to preach and a dwelling in the city of Canterbury, which was the chief city of all his realm".

And didn't they set the pattern which was followed for a thousand years or more? with it good or bad as you've a mind.

"They were constantly at prayer", says Bede, "they fasted and kept vigils, and regarded worldy things as of little importance . . . they assembled to sing the Psalms, to say Mass, to preach, and to baptise, until the King's own conversion gave them greater freedom to preach, and to restore and build churches everywhere".

Mind you, not everybody saw with Bede's kindly eye. Gildas the Wise, a sixth-century monk, buried at Glastonbury, wrote that the English priests were "unworthy wretches, wallowing, after the fashion of swine, in this old and unhappy puddle of intolerable wickedness".

Anyway, saints or sinners, there *are* a few of their churches surviving here and elsewhere: a little chapel at Lullingstone in Kent, dating from the middle of the fourth century, decorated with murals, having something of simplicity . . . or there's the remains of a chapel at Silchester, the old Roman city in Hampshire, small, with the rudiments of an apse at the western end of the nave, aisles, transept, and a stone trough outside in which the faithful washed before entering. Strangely, in the local churchyard there's a sundial whose base is a column looted from a Roman Temple . . . "old stone to new building . . ."

Yes, all time "eternally present".

But the history of the Church is there for all to read . . . and the guide-books will tell you all you need or want to know about those scattered churches.

Where, then, is the holy ground of the early years?

*   *   *

You could do worse than walk the green turf and worn stones of Iona, one of the smaller islands of the Inner Hebrides off the stormy west coast of Scotland, by the Ross of Mull . . . and it famous for St Columba.

True, it was holy before Himself ever set foot on the place, and there's evidence that the Sun was worshipped on Iona in the days of the long ago – as why wouldn't it be? Neil Gunn tells of "three-hundred-and-sixty sculptured stones" which used to stand there, probably Celtic crosses smashed at the Protestant Reformation, making it the Christian sister to Callanish on Lewis.

And then there's a great stone slab outside the door of St Oran's Chapel, you can't miss it: got these three smooth hollows in the top surface. Well, at one time there was a white marble stone in each, and every visitor, man or priest, woman or child, had to turn the three stones round three times sunwise . . . or the Last Trump would sound there and then. Which was bad enough, as who'd be wanting the Day of Judgement before shriving time? But when those stones had worn through the slab with all this turning – well, *then* the Ending of the World by Fire would just as surely come. So you'd be working your own Salvation or slow destruction no matter *what* you did . . . all you had was the choice between the fire or the trumpet. Though isn't choice one of the names of the oldest game in the Book?

Anyway, then there's the Black Stones on which the "Kings of Scotland took their oaths", with the bones of sixty such kings there in the cloister garth until the sounding of that Last Trump – whenever it sounds to their awakening.

And the whole island has always had a mysterious quality that sets it apart . . . perhaps something to do with the clarity of the light, as in Dublin.

Iona begins for Christians in the sixth century with Columba, son of Phelim, of the Royal Irish House of Niall of the Nine Hostages – which is enough of a descent for any man, let alone a Saint of God, so it is.

"Tall, broad, vigorous, tempestuous, with a voice of thunder", writes John Moorman, "he could strike terror into the heart of any who opposed him". And there's a vivid contemporary account: "A typical Irishman, vehement, irrestible . . . hear him curse a niggardly rich man or bless the heifers of a poor peasant . . . see him follow a robber who has plundered a friend, cursing the wretch to his destruction, following him to the water's edge, wading up to his knees in the clear green sea-water, with both hands raised to Heaven".

Wasn't *he* the broth of a boy! And with Columba the Latin name for "dove", so it is!

During his time Ireland was "glittering with Saints who were as numerous as the stars", and he lived his early years studying, copying rare manuscripts, wandering the land on his own two holy feet, teaching, setting up churches and monasteries galore, and, naturally enough, fighting like a true son of his brutal days. Didn't he once take his clans into battle, led by the Archangel Michael, and win a "magnificent triumph", losing only one man, and "slaying three thousand of the enemy, who were Pagans", so he did. Though what the like of that has to do with Jesus Christ would need some explaining.

Which was what the "Saints and Elders of the Irish Church" also thought, because they excommunicated him for the slaughter – though they later relented, and told him to "go out and win as many souls for the Church as had been lost in the battle".

So, eventually, at the prime of forty, he picked eleven companions, and undertook a "pilgrimage to a place out of sight of his beloved Ireland" . . . and set sail in the early Summer of AD563, "heading northwards to the islands off the coast of Western Scotland".

"Set sail" is a brave way of putting it, surely, because a coracle was all they had to be using: a framework of slender branches covered by hides made taut by thongs of leather laced to the top edge of the frame . . . with those seas restless on the best of mornings, and the rocks treacherous every hour, and the distance still weary.

But, after six days and nights, or seven, during the Merry Month of May, they landed in a cove on the south coast of Iona, known to this day as *Port of the Coracle,* when he climbed the nearest hill to be sure of not seeing Ireland . . . with that still known as the *Hill with its Back to Ireland,* a sad enough name for any Irishman, sinner or saint.

From that time to the hour of his mortal death you'd have a fine job to be sifting God's own truth from the legends.

* * *

124

For a start was made when St Oran, one of the eleven companions, offered to be "buried alive" as a "sacrifice" to be making the place holy . . . so they dig him out a grave to his size and chosen depth, and bury him – which was a sad and unholy thing for Saints to be doing.

But then, after three days, what do they do but open it up to see how your man was doing . . . and him alive, so he was.

"There is no such wonder in death", says he, "nor is Hell what it has been described".

"Earth!" says Columba, quick as a sword, "earth on his eyes, lest he further blab!"

And didn't they bury your man again? and him to his chosen depth?

*　　*　　*

Then to the building of their church, with nothing to show this day but the foundations on the little hillock opposite the West door of the present small cathedral, and the last remains of his cell and the naked rock floor on which he slept, his pillow a stone. And then the monastery of beehive-shaped cells of timber and turf, and a refectory, a guest house, fields for the tilling, and dreams and night visions, and the conversion of kings . . . until wasn't Himself one of the greatest of holy men, nettle-soup his only broth, with many miracles to his name, and the Angels in white garments coming on wings from Heaven to be talking with him, and the pilgrims coming long and hazardous journeys from all over Europe to be paying their respects – as why wouldn't they?

*　　*　　*

But then, being a mortal man, he died and was buried . . . and then dug up a century later for to be given a Shrine of silver and gold to his bones, with even more pilgrims coming to pray before these holy relics.

And then the first of the Viking raiders, who plundered and destroyed and murdered, so that the monks fled to the safety of Kells back in Ireland . . . only to return, for there to be more raids and murderings . . .

So back to Kells . . . and the island left deserted . . .

"In Iona of my heart", had Columba foretold, "in Iona of my love, instead of the voices of monks shall be the lowing of cattle . . . but, ere the world come to an end, Iona shall be as it was".

Well, Himself has been dead before the High Altar of the Abbey these fourteen centuries . . . and, though Iona is not *quite* as it was, aren't the pilgrims still coming?

Two hundred thousand a year, with yourself more than welcome.

"For", says Sam Johnson to James Boswell, themselves visitors in their own times, "that man is little to be envied", says he, "whose piety would not grow warmer among the ruins of Iona". And them Protestants!

True, it's not so easy as it used to be to have your piety warmed, for there are the ferries bringing the tourists across from Mull, the steamers from elsewhere . . . and the gift-shop and tea-room, the hotel and the . . . yes, the golf-course . . .

Yet *there* are the wildflowers growing in the joints and crannies of the ruined walls, and the weathered Celtic crosses, and the worn stones and tombs, the carvings and the memories, the Well of the North Wind and the Well of Eternal Youth, the Ross of Mull across the water, and the Bay of Martyrs where the Vikings had the slaughtering of sixty-eight, and the White Strand of the Monks where the later Norsemen had the slaughtering of sixteen more . . . so that you have the salt passion of the ocean before you, the sky of Heaven above your head, with the white doves of the Abbey swirling, and the bones of the ancient dead beneath your feet.

All you need is to be there in a time of your own choosing . . . and to stay longer in the Chapel of St Oran than in the Cathedral, for plain white-washed walls and a silver Celtic Cross are closer to Christ than many more ornate furnishing, however beautiful. And wasn't it Oran Himself who thought "no such wonder in death", and knew that Hell could hold no terrors for those who believe in the powers of Heaven . . . and can't we be doing with such blessed assurance these days, surely?

And please have a look at the modern bronze sculpture of the Virgin Mary in the Cloisters, because it was made by Jacob Lipchitz, a "Jew faithful to the Faith of his Fathers", for a

126

"good understanding among all the people of the earth", and that the "Spirit may reign".

So there's many a yard of holy ground . . .

"Yes", wrote Mendelssohn, and him after hearing the music of Fingal's Cave, "when in some future time I shall sit in a madly crowded assembly, and the wish arises in me to return into the loneliest loneliness, I shall think of Iona . . ."

Though, the truth being the truth, you'd have another fine job to be lonely there on any high day of Summer these recent years.

With the last words being those of Columba: "Delightful I think it to be in the bosom of the isle", says he, "on the peak of a rock, that I might often watch there the calm of the sea . . . its heavy waves over the glittering ocean . . . hear", says he, "the sound of the shallow waves against the rocks . . . the very noise of the sea . . . its ebb and its flood-tide in their flow . . ."

And, surely, that same sea off Iona can be as calm for us as it ever was for Himself, the waves as glittering . . . for, truly, the "sea has many voices, many gods and many voices".

And bring back a pebble from the beach with you, dark red or dull yellow or green serpentine, white veined or speckled, smooth from that sea, and hold it in your hand when you've a mind to . . . and remember . . .

*   *   *

Or there, on the other side of the country altogether, just south of the Scottish Borders, about a mile off the Northumberland Coast, is the Holy Isle of Lindisfarne, and it first made holy by St Aiden in the seventh century . . . and him a Scot from where else than Iona?

"A bishop of outstanding gentleness, holiness, and moderation", says Bede, "much given to humility and holy poverty" . . . to whom King Oswald of Northumbria, "a man beloved of God", granted the island as a base for the reconversion of the kingdom. "As the tide ebbs and flows", says Bede, "this place is surrounded by sea twice a day, and twice a day the sand dries and joins it to the mainland" . . . with it doing the same to this day, and life there dominated by the tides – so you'll need to manage the time of your arrival just as they did.

But wasn't your man the grand example for many a modern bishop, for he "loved to give way to the poor who chanced to meet him whatever he received from kings or wealthy folk", says Bede, "and he always travelled on foot unless compelled by necessity to ride". More, "if wealthy people did wrong, he never kept silent out of respect or fear . . ."

Great days, surely . . . and his gaunt bronze backs a Celtic Cross there for every eye to see.

Not that he could have lived many of his days on Lindisfarne, for he was always travelling hither and yon, preaching, doing good, "cultivating peace and love, purity and humility", being "above anger and greed", despising "pride and conceit", comforting the sick, "relieving and protecting the poor". And him drawing his last breath miles away on the mainland, by the side of a church – and where better place for a bishop?

And not that there's much left of his work on Lindisfarne . . . for the first monastery was sacked by the Danes at the end of the eighth century, and again in the middle of the ninth, with them being perilous times for more than monks. "From the wrath of the Northmen", was the prayer of the Church, "O Lord, protect us".

The present ruins are those of the Benedictine Priory built in the eleventh century, the legend telling how the masons and carpenters were "supplied with bread which came out of the air and wine which flowed from an inexhaustible chalice" . . . destroyed and looted by Thomas Cromwell's men in the sixteenth . . . rain and sea-winds doing the rest.

Alas! as with Iona, it's imagination you need to walk with St Aidan at all . . . for there's the narrow concrete causeway across the low tide, and the cars bumper-to-bumper . . . there are the icecream-vans, and tins of Coke and Pepsi . . . and *there* are the bottles of genuine Lindisfarne Mead . . . the fagends and empty cigarette-packets . . .

And yet there are the screaming gulls, those wildflowers again, the drenched grass, the grey-green sea along the beach, drifts of pebbles scrunching underfoot, the same sort and shapes as he would have known, the wild wind driving the same urgencies of cloud . . . and *there*, to the south-east, are the Farne Islands, a place of seals and sea-birds . . .

So come your own way at another time of your own choosing.

*   *   *

Or why not visit the British Museum in London, and ask to look at the Lindisfarne Gospels?

For they came from the first monastery, copied from the Latin of St Jerome, written and illuminated on vellum at the end of the seventh century: "Eadfrith, Bishop of the Brethren at Lindisfarne, he at the first scripted this book for God and St Cuthbert and for all the Saints in common that are on the island, and Ethilwald bound and covered it outwardly as well as he could. And Billfrith and Anchorite, he wrought as a smith the ornaments that are on the outside and adorned it with gold and with gems, also with silver overgilded, a treasure without peer. And Afred, an unworthy and most miserable priest, with God's help and St Cuthbert's, over-glossed it in English . . ."

Most of the pages are plain calligraphy – that is, some of the most beautiful handwriting ever done – just the decorated initial capitals here and there like small jewels. The main glories are at the beginning of each Gospel, where the whole page is covered by interlacing patterns of spirals and boughs and branches and birds and beasts and flowers and faces, filled with all manner of mystery and colours . . . and the Word.

It was once washed into the sea and lost . . . and then found, stranded along the beach of a distant coast . . .

Legend?

On its pages are the stains of sea-water.

*   *   *

Another monk of Lindisfarne was St Cuthbert, born near Melrose Abbey, Berwickshire, in the middle of the seventh century – and him brought up to be a shepherd. Well, there he was, watching his flocks by night on the Lammermuir Hills, like many other shepherd before him, and quite a few since, when a "bright shining ray of light shone down from Heaven" . . . he heard "Choirs of Angels singing", and had a Vision of other Angels "giving welcome to a human soul" and "bearing it in triumph to the Divine Presence".

And then, when he told all this to his parents, and the priests got to hear about it, he discovered that St Aidan had died at that "same hour of the night" . . . so it must have been *his* soul the Angels were welcoming. As why wouldn't they?

So what did he do but up and away to Melrose on the banks of the River Tweed for to become a monk himself? Knocked on the door, and asked to be let in out of the world. "Behold", said the Porter on the gate, "the Servant of the Lord". And in he walked . . . though he wasn't allowed the peace he craved, for off he was soon sent on his journeyings, this way and that place, preaching and healing, in all winds and every weather, over moors and through forests, taking the Good News of Salvation to all who would hear and many who wouldn't.

And aren't there the lovely stories about the man?

There he was, staying at this monastery or that priory, when a monk saw him stealing away out one shining moonlit night, and followed him for to watch what would happen. And Cuthbert walked down to the beach of the sea, and stripped himself to his shivering skin, and waded into the waves of that bitterly cold water . . . where he stood all the hours until dawn, praising God with Psalms and other songs.

This was a common enough mortification, and whole choirs of monks would "immerse themselves in the icy sea all night, chanting litanies through chattering teeth".

But when Cuthbert waded back, he had these two seals slithering up the sands behind him, where they breathed on his feet to warm them, and waited for his blessing before returning to their dark green depths.

And another time he was fed in a wilderness place by an eagle . . . with many a wild creature his friend, and none to harm.

But then, after twelve years or thirteen of these wanderings, he craved once more for the peace of solitude, no sound but the waves and the cries of sea-birds . . . and he was allowed to leave for Lindisfarne, where he lived happy days and contemplative nights close to his wild creatures, and closer to God. Yet even the solitude of a cell among other cells wasn't what his soul craved – so what did he do but up and away to those outer Farne Islands down the coast? Where he dug himself a cell down in the rock, and made a low wall around it "just so high that he could see nothing but the Heavens for which he longed so ardently", and a roof of thatch over . . . and there he settled, his only view those Heavens, his only companions the seals, his friends the gulls.

"Where", says Bede, "he lived a solitary life in great self-mastery of mind and body".

Though he had trouble with a pair of crows, or it might have been ravens, who pulled out straws from his thatch for their nest . . . so he asked them, reasonably enough, to leave him his roof intact against the rain. But they couldn't resist the ease of it, and the straws so convenient, with them pulling more . . . so he banished them from the island – as why wouldn't he?

But then didn't the poor creatures come straggling back, their wings trailing and their heads low, and them croaking for pardon?

And wasn't he quick to grant it? with his conscience a burden to him since they'd gone.

Well, legend or not, there's a truth about the man of flesh behind the gold and silver fancy-work . . . for there can be little holiness where creatures are not loved, less goodness where they're harmed, and no happiness when they're never given a second thought. With the world a better home for us all when they're allowed their proper place in it.

*   *   *

But then King Egfrid of Northumbria, and the "most holy bishop Trumwine", came out to Farne for to make *him* a bishop . . . and off he was obliged to wander again, this way and to Hexham, and from there to far elsewhere, preaching and healing for for Salvation of men and women, never forgetting their children.

Until, full of years and wanderings, yearning for death and those Angels of welcome, he was once more allowed to depart in peace for Lindisfarne and his cell on that outer island of seals and gulls . . . where his "fastings were exceptional", because he "spent his last days subsisting on a few dried onions to support the frail life in his body". And, naturally enough, soon died . . . though not before "earnestly requesting the brethren to bury him in this place where he had served God for so long".

Well, they buried him back on Lindisfarne, in a stone tomb to the right of the High Altar . . . and *that* should have been the end of his far wanderings and wide.

But he fetched up in Durham four hundred years later, so he did . . . with that yet another legend, and now not the proper time for the telling of it.

⋆   ⋆   ⋆

Though St Cuthbert wasn't the only one of these Celtic and Saxon Saints to crave solitude, not all were so wholesome . . . and even *he* couldn't stand the sight nor sound of women. "Which seems out of character", murmurs a charitable commentator.

In depressing fact, none of them had much time for women and the holy pleasures of the flesh, with celibacy their daily struggle, and fearful stories to be told at any time. And not merely of struggles against the very thought of woman as the "real Satan, the foe of peace", but against the flesh itself, male or female.

"When you hath once been washed in Christ", wrote St Jerome, "there is no need that you should ever again wash . . . So do not complain that thy skin, without washing, is rough and wrinkled". St Etheldred of Ely, for one among tens of thousands, "bathed only thrice a year", for "she who was so clean-washed in heart needed not to be washed in body". And most of them "enjoyed" living in their own filth, called lice "the pearls of Heaven", wore knotted hair-shirts and rusting chains until their flesh rotted . . . and "offered up their mortifications" to God "in recompense for the sins of the world".

All things "beautiful to the eye, soft to the ear, agreeable to the smell, sweet to the taste, and pleasant to the touch", wrote St Bernard of Clairvaux, "must be accounted dross and dung" . . . and even the slightly more balanced St Anselm advised that "the delight of the senses is rarely good, mostly bad".

They were desperate about "controlling the belly", and would fast for weeks on end – and then eat only "dry bread and salt", with a "little brackish water". Or "eat salt and drink no water . . ."

Or they would go without sleep, or pray for hours with arms wide out-stretched, or remain silent for a lifetime . . . all to teach the innocent body that *it* was the source of sin.

But it was women, "vile sewers, bags of filth, the spawn of Hell", who troubled them most, and the lengths they would go to avoid "lascivious" thoughts are tokens of sick minds: they would "chastise" themselves and each other with multi-thonged whips, scourges, flails, birch-rods . . . and then leave the wounds and weals to fester. One man, saint or sinner, with a woman sheltering from a storm in the doorway of his cell, "burned his fingers joint by joint in the flame of a lamp to defeat the fire of lust" – and *then* had the wickedness to call her a "child of Hell" for tempting him. Others "rolled naked in thorns" to conquer what was obviously the unconquerable, and then "lashed themselves with rods" for "enjoying the pain of the thorns".

St Ailred, Abbot of the Cistercian Monastery of Rievaulx during the twelfth century, had an idea of his own: he had built a "small chamber of brick under the floor of the Novice House, like a little cistern, into which water flowed from hidden streams". When he was "alone and undisturbed" he'd "enter this place, and immerse his whole body in the icy cold water and so quench the heat in himself of every vice". Though at least he'd be clean.

These are the "Holy Virgins" who thought of little else except their own sexual deprivation, the "pure" wallowing in their own nastiness, returning again and again to the "sins" they condemned and yet so vicariously enjoyed by describing in fascinated detail . . . wrecks of human-beings, stunted, de-formed, barren, failures even by their own twisted and inadequate standards. With seven devils to surge back into their unhealthy souls, being far more unclean than the one "driven out" by such sado-masochism, their "last state worse than their first" . . . the gentle gift of Love demanding a terrible price for its rejection.

What abiding beauty of holiness can come from clogged and putrifying sewers?

Consider St Guthlac . . .

*　　*　　*

Late seventh century, a contemporary of St Cuthbert, he was the son of a Mercian nobleman, Penwald, and Tette, his wife . . . and the story of his life was told by Felix, a Saxon chronicler.

In his youth he was a soldier, taking part in all the usual brutality of those perilous times, and was even "famous" . . . but, at the age of twenty-four, he "sought refuge" in the Abbey of Repton in Derbyshire. After two years "the desire came over him for a more secluded life" . . . and he heard about an "island in the Fens of Lincolnshire", south of the Wash, "which seemed to be the very spot he was seeking".

So, at the turning of the century, he "landed on the island of Croyland", not much more than a "slight rise in the surrounding flatness", found the "sow with a litter of white pigs" under the "willow-tree" as "revealed in a dream" to be the place, built a small wattle-hut of a hermitage . . . and died in it "during Passion Week" fourteen years later.

The Fens were "dismal swamps" in those days, the "ague and all the attendant sickness of a low-lying country assailed" him, the "wind cut keenly across the waste", the "few inhabitants" were "rough and barbaric" . . . and he "ascribed all these trials as personal attacks upon him by the Powers of Darkness and Evil".

He "sought the help of St Bartholomew", on whose Festival Day he had landed, was taken up to Heaven in either Vision or fact, and "obtained in answer to his prayer a three-thonged whip" . . . which, says a sadly sympathetic commentator, "is a grim reminder of one of the hazards of the solitary life – the temptations of the flesh".

It's all too depressing to bear thinking about for long: that sick, partly crazed, perhaps even demented man, cold, hungry, thirsty, avoiding the company of his fellow men, lashing his own dirty body with that "whip of discipline" in a vain attempt to prevent himself from even thinking about women . . . all for the "Greater Glory of God".

His cell is still just about there, was excavated in 1908, covered in again, with its position marked by a metal label to the west of the south aisle of the ruins which remain from former magnificence.

Because a great Benedictine Abbey grew from that small wattle hut.

First a wooden church with a roof of thatch, looted and destroyed by maurauding Danes, who carried off that "treasured whip and the Psalter of the Saint". Then a stone building, fires, raids, rebuilding . . . until, by Norman times, there was a solid enough Church and Monastery . . . then another fire, another transformation into the Perpendicular style . . . and then came Thomas Cromwell's men.

The north aisle is used today as the Parish church, the little market town is remote, the area drained and no longer an island, but still bleak, and is obviously no great centre of contemporary pilgrimage . . . and yet the sky is vast, and there's a "cold clarity" to it, the distances wide and reaching, the sense of space invigorating.

So, in mercy and pity, spare a thought for our Brother Guthlac.

Below that metal label lies the floor of his cell:

Died A.D. 714 R.I.P.

Patch of stale earth, a rose straggling in the wind off the Fens, crumblings of stone fallen from the walls, a few pigeon feathers, droppings, weeds, three fagends, an empty cigarette-packet . . .

A car roared by, radio blaring Pop . . .

Then silence, blessed silence.

"Learn how to wait", he's supposed to have said, "and the Kingdom of Heaven shall come unto thee".

Patience, then . . .

★   ★   ★

Not that they were *all* given to those self-defeating austerities.

136

One lovely and loving saint was called by Bede a "Holy man named John", and the simplicity of the tribute is reflected in the simple human goodness of his life. And there can be little of legend in it, because Bede knew him well – indeed, had been ordained Deacon and then Priest by him. So it's a relief to be dealing with flesh and blood rather than gilded plaster.

Not a lot known about his early years, but he'd founded a monastery at In-Derawuda, meaning "in the wood of the Deiri", with that Northern tribe occupying what is now part of South Yorkshire. And he was bishop of Hexham towards the end of the seventh century . . . and Bede describes one incident in his life which will have to serve for many, all of them moving, full of love and his gentle compassion.

Seems that every Lent, which was the same season of prayer and fasting then as it used to be until recently, starting with Ash Wednesday and lasting until the High Glories of Easter, this John used to "retire with a few companions" to an isolated place "surrounded by open woodland", where they'd study and pray. Well, this particular time, "as was his invariable custom", he "requested his companions to find some poor person who was seriously infirm or in dire want", for to "live with them during their stay" . . . and they found a "dumb youth" who had "never been able to utter a single word". More than that, "he had so many scabs and scales on his head that no hair ever grew on the crown, but only a few wisps stood up in a ragged circle round it".

And this "poor lad" came to John, who then, patiently, with no instant miracle, taught him to speak, first the letters, then the words . . . and the "lad's tongue was loosed", so that he spoke "sentences and longer sentences". With this most moving and completely convincing passage: "All those who were present say that the next day and the next night, as long as he could keep awake, the youth never stopped saying something and expressing his inner thoughts and wishes to others . . ." As, Glory be to God, why wouldn't he?

John was "delighted, and directed the physician to undertake the cure of the youth's scabby head" . . . and the skin "healed, and a vigorous growth of hair appeared".

In the words of William Purcell: "There is a ring of truth here . . . (the lad) needed only a little kindness to make him whole".

And that was John all over: never asking God to do what he could perfectly well do for himself . . . though "always remembering the source of all goodness".

Well, the "Holy man named John" eventually became bishop of York, went about doing his more practical sort of healing and comforting for thirty-three years, then "retired to his original monastery" at In-Derawuda, and "ended his days in a manner pleasing to God".

With In-Derawuda now being the small town of Beverley in Humberside . . . where there's a Minster, "in size and splendour more than the equal of some cathedrals" . . . and yet, mysteriously, his simplicity still manages to survive. For he's buried there, and it shows.

The usual tale of small beginnings, destruction by the Danes in the eighth century, rebuilding on a larger scale, a fire in the twelfth century, an even larger and more magnificent building . . . then the central tower collapsed in the thirteenth century . . . more rebuilding "mainly on Gothic lines" during the next two hundred years . . .

With, all the time, his tomb drawing the pilgrims . . . though it soon became a Shrine, "gleaming in finest gold and shining of fairest silver". It stood at the apex of a screen behind the High Altar . . . but, of course, it was looted during the Protestant Reformation. You can still see where it used to be, and trace the steps of the pilgrims if you've a mind.

But I can't really believe that Holy John of Beverley would

have been much impressed by any of it . . . though I'm sure he'd smile in tears as the children of his native village of Harpham on the Wolds, where he was born thirteen centuries ago, come dandering in every year on his birthday during the Merry Month of May to deck his grave-slab with primroses of their own gathering.

You're never far from holiness with wildflowers.

*　　*　　*

And then there's Brother Caedmon . . . though *his* story is almost too well-known for the telling. Except that it's new every morning with the dew on the green grass, and him still singing down the arches of the years to us from that time when our language was in the April of its long year.

Seventh century, like the others, sinners or saints, and him a cowman, or a shepherd, or a keeper of pigs – as though it matters. Unlettered, that's what matters, with him neither reading nor writing a word of his own for the length of his days. For it was only the bishops and priests who were the clerks, the clerics, only the monks the scribes . . . and the men and women who worked the land and the loom, who delved and spun, smelted and sawed and hammered – *these* never had the learning of such high matters. And even the languages of learning were Greek and Latin, with the words of the people too uncouth for anything more holy than holy living and holier dying.

With all this down the coast from Lindisfarne, at Streanaeshalch, called the Bay of the Beacon . . . or Whitby as we know it today, there being a great Abbey in all its pomp up on those cliffs, St Hilda the Abbess, a library of manuscripts, and the place important enough to hold the Synod at which was settled the bitter disputes between the Celtic Church and the Roman about such matters as the correct date for Easter and the proper form of tonsure for priests and monks . . .

"Glory be!" I can hear St Columba saying, had he been spared the hundred years. "The Northmen are after destroying us, and you talking about the phases of the moon and the hairs of your heads!"

Well, there was Caedmon working at this Abbey, a son of the people . . . so what would *he* know about such things? How could *he* sing the Songs of Zion at all?

And so, with Bede doing the telling, "when it happened at a feast . . ."

Meat or fish, dried peas or beans, bread and ale, perhaps apples and berries had it been Autumn.

"When it happened at a feast", says Bede, "that everybody in turn would be invited to sing and entertain the company, then Caedmon would leave the table before the harp came his way, and go to his bed".

Not that the harp was the instrument we now know, all those strings and pedals and shimmerings of sound – but a few strings on a small and simple frame, with the rhythm counting more than any melody, the beat and the surge of the verse being the master of this music, the pauses and stresses its mystery.

"At one such time", says Bede, "he left the table before the harp came his way, and went out to the barn, it being his duty that night to look after the beasts".

And the barn of rough wood, thatched with reeds or turf, and the floor of trodden mud.

"When the work was done", says Bede, "and the time came, he settled down to sleep".

And his bed of planks, raised from the ground for the damp and the rats . . . with rags for his coverings.

"Suddenly", says Bede, "in a dream he saw a man standing beside him. . . ."

And the man called him by name: "Caedmon", says he, "sing me a song".

"I know not how", says Caedmon. "It is because I cannot

sing that I left the feast".

"But", says the man, "you shall sing to me".

"What shall I sing?" says Caedmon.

"Sing about the Creation of all things", says the man.

"And immediately", says Bede, "Caedmon began to sing in praise of God the Creator . . ."

The words as fresh this morning as they were that night:

"Praise we and Worship now the Warden of Heaven,
The Majesty of His Might and His Mind's Wisdom.
Work of the World-Warden, Worker of all Wonders.
How He, the Lord of Glory everlasting,
Wrought first for Earth's Children the Heavens for a Roof.
Then made He Middle Earth to be their Mansion . . ."

"This is the sense", says Bede, "but not the actual words that Caedmon sang in his dream, for these cannot be translated from his language without losing much of their beauty and dignity".

From Anglo-Saxon into the Latin prose of Bede, and from that into our English . . . and yet something remains. Indeed, in one of the manuscripts those lines have also been copied from some Anglo-Saxon source . . . so we are closer to Caedmon.

"Early in the morning", says Bede, "he went to his Reeve, being the manager of the Abbey's estate, and told him about this gift he had received. And the Reeve took him before the Abbess Hilda, who requested of him to give an account of his dream and to repeat the song in the presence of many learned men. And all of them agreed that this gift had been given him by Our Lord". As why wouldn't they?

"The Abbess was delighted that God had given such grace to the man", says Bede, "and ordered him to be instructed in Sacred History, and Caedmon stored up in his memory all that he learnt", says Bede, "and turned it into such melodious song that he made his teachers into his audience".

And there he was, from that day to the day of his mortal death, a son of the people teaching his people in their own language . . . the first of our own Poets.

And what were the songs he sang?

"He sang of the Creation of the world", says Bede, "of the Promised Land, the Lord's Incarnation, Passion, Resurrection, and Ascension into Heaven, the Coming of the Holy Spirit, and the teaching of the Apostles".

And the greatest of these was *The Dream of the Rood*:
        "I looked on the Rood, arrayed in glory,
        Shining in beauty, gilded with gold,
        Lustrous with jewels. Yet I saw plainly
        How grim ones had gashed it.
        Down from its sides the red drops were trickling,
        Now wet and stained,
        Now fairly jewelled with gold and with gems . . ."
And then Caedmon crowned his life with a happy end: "Having served God with a simple and pure mind", says Bede, "he left the world and departed to Heaven by a tranquil death. For his tongue", says Bede, "which had sung so much in praise of his Master, uttered its last words in that same praise, and commended his soul into that Heavenly keeping".

With after that the usual story: the whole place destroyed by the Danes in the ninth century, left desolate until the eleventh, rebuilt as a Benedictine Abbey, destroyed by Thomas Cromwell's men during the sixteenth . . . and now, it says here, "admirably maintained by the Department of the Environment".

Yes, a high wall of breeze-blocks around, and turnstiles at the gates, cars and icecream-vans on the green grass outside . . . yet that sea is the same as for Brother Caedmon, that Bay of the Beacon, those cliffs, the Westering sun going down over the far headland . . .

And when the tide is swelling the buoy at the entrance to the little harbour heaves and rolls . . . and the bell booms distantly . . . almost as though the vanished bells of the Abbey were ringing a Requiem under the sea . . . measuring a "time not our time . . ."

Yes, it is still possible to look on the Rood with Caedmon at Whitby.

★   ★   ★

"This, then", says our other Brother, the Venerable Bede, at the end of his History, "is the present state of Britain, seven-hundred-and-thirty years since Our Lord's Incarnation . . . Let the multitude of isles be glad thereof, and give thanks at the remembrance of His holiness!"

Amen to that . . . and peace to your travelled relics.

Monks and Masons

And then, we are told, came the Age of Faith, all those monks and nuns, the monasteries and abbeys and their great churches, the early cathedrals ... for they had long since destroyed the living groves, and now built these forests of stone.

But, first, peace to some other travelled relics.

Remember St Cuthbert?

Well, now's the proper time for the telling of his wanderings ... not those of his life, but of his body after his death.

* * *

He died on Farne Island, and wanted to rest where he'd served God so long – but his Brethren buried him back on Lindisfarne, in a tomb of stone by the High Altar ... and the miracles started, healings and other wonders, and the pilgrims began to arrive.

So his Brethren, with a natural enough view to be having him better seen, opened his tomb ... and his body hadn't corrupted: the grand miracle, surely, needing a Shrine.

But then came the Danes ... and the Brethren fled, taking the miraculous body and other treasures with them, over hill and down dale, through the dark woods of this world, fording rivers and climbing mountains, many a weary and long mile.

Sir Walter Scott is less than sympathetic: "The Saint was a most capricious fellow-traveller, which was the more intolerable, as, like Sinbad's Old Man of the Sea, he journeyed upon the shoulders of his companions. They paraded him through Scotland for several years, and came as far West as Withern, in Galloway, whence they attempted to sail for Ireland, but were driven back by tempests".

Which was where the Lindisfarne Gospels were washed into the sea and lost, to be found stranded along the beach of a distant shore ...

"He at length made a halt at Norham", says Scott, "from thence he went to Melrose, where he remained stationary for a

145

short time, and then caused himself to be launched upon the Tweed in a stone coffin . . ."

And on they went, "gathering many gifts of land and riches in honour of the Saint", fetching up in Yorkshire, and then Chester-le-Street in Northumbria, where a Shrine was built . . . and here they settled for a hundrd years or more, with Himself growing in fame and themselves in wealth. Until, at the end of the tenth century, the Danes . . . so it was away again with the body and the treasures of Ripon, six years or seven there, and to the North again . . .

But, doubtless having had enough and to be sparing, Himself "revealed in a dream" that he wanted to rest at a "place called Dunholme" . . . which was now their command.

Except where in the land was Dunholme?

Then they heard two women talking about the "lost cow strayed into the Dunholme" . . . and wasn't it the woods in a loop of the River Wear? And it now Durham, so it is.

And *there*, after three hundred years of his wanderings in death, they built a small church of wood for to be resting him while they started a cathedral of stone for his last Shrine . . . with the pilgrims arriving, the gifts gathering.

By now the Normans had conquered, and were "putting down tumults" all over the place and marching North . . . so off fled the Brethren back to Lindisfarne, lugging the body and all they could carry with them.

But, eventually, they returned to Durham at the end of the eleventh century, finished what they had to finish of their stone cathedral . . . and then, *then*, at the beginning of the twelfth century, after another look at how he was getting on his coffin (when they found a sixth-century St John's Gospel they'd somehow missed before), they moved him into that "splended Shrine which he was to occupy throughout the long years of the Middle Ages", with his body, after several more examinations, still not corrupt, "complete and even flexible . . ."

Which was miracle enough for any pilgrims, surely . . . and they came in their thousands and tens of thousands, and continued to come for the next few hundred years.

★   ★   ★

It's interesting to remember the standards by which the Church judged a state of "incorruption" during that Age of Faith.

St Clare, for example, Beloved Spiritual Sister of St Francis, had her body "miraculously preserved" after her death, and it's still venerated at Assisi.

"I found myself gazing in horror at it through a glass-topped coffin", wrote Karen Armstrong, a Roman Catholic nun for seven years. "The face is black, wizened, rather like a monkey's. Her hands are gnarled and skeletal. This so-called miracle was meant to lift the mind to God, but does no more than present a pathetic portrait of pickled humanity. Poor St Clare, she should be put decently away, not exposed to the prurient gaze of chance spectators".

Anyway, when Cuthbert was examined for what we hope is the last time at the beginning of this century, he was in his robes ... but reduced to bones, which were "put decently away" for good, and the grave sealed.

Rest in Peace.

When does the looting of graves become archeology?

★   ★   ★

With those Normans the first of the great builders in England, monks and masons out-Romaning the Romans, all those squared stones and round arches, solid columns and dark crypts . . . with King William founding Battle Abbey in immediate thanksgiving for the Conquest, and it where the battle was won, the High Altar on the very yard of Saxon earth where Harold Godwinson fell, that arrow destroying his eye to his mortal death. And that Abbey remains to this day in picture-postcard decrepitude – with many another elsewhere, larger or smaller, in similar decay or daily use, neglected or restored ... "bare ruined choirs where late the sweet birds sang" or still loud with Choral Evensong.

And there they all are for the visiting: Abbeys, Cathedrals, Chapels, Churches, Friaries, Monasteries, and assorted Priories ... from Westminster to St Albans and Bury St Edmunds, Norwich to Leicester by way of Walsingham and Peterborough, from Southwell to Lincoln and from Beverley to York and Whitby and Lindisfarne, and back by way of Durham and Rievaulx and Ripon and Fountains, Kirkstall and Tintern and Gloucester, Wells and Glastonbury and Salisbury and Winchester, even Aylesford and unto Canterbury ...

And what wonders of wood and stone, such images of gold and silver and bronze and sounding brass, such glories and magnificence ...

Yes, the approach to Canterbury along the Pilgrim's Way, that Constable view of Salisbury Cathedral across the water-meadows with my Lord Bishop out for a stroll with his Lady, the "joy of elevated thoughts" above Tintern Abbey, those dramatic square towers of Durham and the great round piers of the Nave with their patterns which go back to New Grange ... the Five Sisters of York celebrated by Charles Dickens in Nicholas Nickleby ... Edward the Confessor's Tomb, Lady Julian's Cell, even the "holy blissful Martyr" Himself ...

Except who could possibly have the time for every last one? who has the days to be travelling? the money to be sparing? the life so long?

Walk your own way . . . find among them your own yard of holy ground.

But here are a few personal colour-transparencies . . . picture-postcards from my own wanderings.

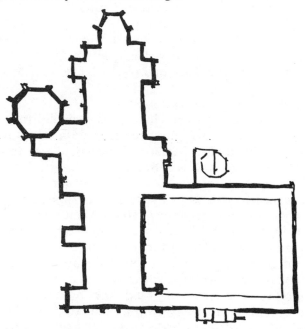

To start at this arbitrary beginning . . .

That they destroyed the living groves is true: we have evidence and no doubt . . . for how many of us remember the *Sweet Cauldron of the Five Trees?* or know who dies each year on St John's Day? or can distinguish any difference between the evergreen scarlet oak and the terebinth?

And yet did they then build forests of stone?

Merely consider Southwell Minster in Nottinghamshire: "a textbook illustration of three successive styles of architecture". Twelfth-century Norman, early thirteenth-century English – with the "chief glory" a Chapter House in the second style of English Decorated Gothic.

But from *what* century does *that* really come?

"The exquisite octagonal Chapter House", it says here, "was

constructed in the late thirteenth century".

Well, yes, that's when the place was built, the stone carved . . . but there are far earlier voices whispering, eyes watching that are "dark as holly", shadows, "teeth made of thorns . . ."

All the rest of the place is standard guide-book: "Nothing of the early Saxon church remains except the doorway in the West wall of the North transept, and a fragment of tessellated paving . . . Note the massive Norman piers and lofty triorium . . . triple arcading at the West end of the Nave . . . The splendid brass lectern . . ."

Read one, and you've read them all.

Except for that Chapter House, traditionally the room in which monks met daily for necessary administration, after which a "chapter of their Monastic Rule would be read aloud" – hence the name. However, at Southwell it was intended for the use of the clergy in the conduct of the Minster's business.

You walk from the North aisle of the Choir, along a short covered passage, turn right through the Vestibule . . . and there you are, back among the groves, surrounded on seven sides by stone trees, slender trunks curving upwards and arching overhead in ribbed branches, budding into carved foliage, leaves and flowers and fruit . . . the oak and its acorns, vines and their grapes, the hawthorn and the blackthorn and the whitethorn, the maple, ivy twining and trailing, the cherry, wormwood, woody nightshade, roses, buttercups, bryony . . .

And those eyes, watching, staring . . . because there, peering from behind and between the leaves, are the demons, the monsters, the dragons, the basilisks, their tails writhing, claws clutching . . . lions, goats, a ram, a bull, wild boars, a hare being torn to pieces by hounds . . . human heads grinning and grimacing . . .

And *there*, again and again, the Green Man of the Woods . . .

How long is time when time has stopped?

For the Green Man is the ancient incarnation of fertility, the Oak-King killed each year on what is now St John's Day, sacrificed when His strength was waning so that the Divine Spirit could be released from His body of flesh, to reincarnate in a revitalised form, and thus spread His life-giving powers throughout the land.

"The belief that kings possess magical or supernatural powers", wrote Sir James Frazer in *The Golden Bough,* "by virtue of which they can fertilise the earth... has left clear traces of itself in our country down to modern times".

If you're a Monarchist or a happy Pagan, then why not?

But what's the Green Man doing in a Christian church?

✶   ✶   ✶

Not that Southwell Minster is the only cathedral or church you'll find him.

Indeed, most cathedrals (especially those in the Perpendicular style) can be seen as groves, cool stone forests with their trees the columns, tall, smooth, straight, their boughs arching overhead, interlacing into fan-vaulting, the high tangle of branches carved with leaves... and there, at the far end of the track between those arches, the sun is shining and shimmering between that tracery, the glimpsed sky intensely blue, the leaves green, the berries scarlet... or is it really only stained-glass?

In other words, some powerful elements of that Ancient Religion, already old when Christianity was young, survived well into the Middle Ages. It's easy to see why, because the Church wasn't yet the dominant social force it was to become, and hadn't much real influence on the deep beliefs and old customs of ordinary people. Indeed, as we've seen, the early missionaries were advised by Pope Gregory that the Pagan Temples "should on no account be destroyed", and that "days

151

of Dedication or the Festivals of the Holy Martyrs" should be substituted in the place of "sacrifices" . . . with Christmas merely being the best-known of these substitutions: the Birth of Christ for the Rebirth of the Sun at the Winter Solstice.

And, according to the unorthodox scholar, Margaret Murray, even some "nobles and clergy successfully managed to combine the old and new religions . . . publicly appearing as devout Christians" while continuing to "observe the practices of the ancient order". And many people now consider that the "annual sacrifice of the king, or a priestly substitute", persisted until at least Norman times.

Documentary evidence is sparse, because it was Christian monks who wrote the histories – and you could hardly expect them to be objective about what they regarded as "Devilish" customs . . . but the most obvious example is that of William Rufus.

★ ★ ★

Son of William the Conqueror, he became King at his father's death in 1087, "openly proclaimed himself a Pagan", missed few opportunities to "deride the Christians" . . . and who, at the end of a Sacred cycle of seven years, was, as the *Anglo-Saxon Chronicle* puts it, "shot off with an arrow from his own man" in the New Forest on the last of the four annual festivals of the Pagan year – which, as we've also seen, remains a "substituted" feast of the Church as Lammas.

All the known details confirm the ritual nature of the sacrifice: he prepared for it in the morning by "arranging the continuity of rule after his death", presented a "pair of new arrows" to the chosen huntsman, instructed him to "do justice according to those things" which he had been told, then entered the forest of great old oaks . . . and was shot with an arrow. "Without a word", he calmly broke off the end, "and fell upon the projecting shaft to die quickly".

So "his blood spilled" on English soil, "due ritual had been observed", and it all took place in a forest glade . . . with his successor, Henry, crowned King at Westminster within three days.

★ ★ ★

And there are many people who are persuaded that Thomas à Becket, the "holy blissful Martyr" of Canterbury, was one of these voluntary sacrificial victims – a "major example of the Divine substitute" being a priest of the new religion.

The pattern is much less obvious than with William Rufus, but, reading between and behind the Christian lines, there are distinctive ritual elements in the timing and manner of his death: Thomas foretold it in his Sermon on Christmas Day, King Henry (whose "death" Thomas was about to die) issued the instructions, the four chosen knights met with the sacrificial victim on the afternoon of the seventh day after the Winter Solstice, he "assured them" that "he would not flee", waited at the altar of the Lady Chapel in the North Transept, the knights entered the Cloisters at the "appointed hour of sunset", Thomas "commended himself to the Doom of God and Mary and the Blessed Dionysius" . . . and then, "serenely", stretched his neck forward, and the knights slew him with their swords, "four blows to spill his blood upon the ground".

And, significantly for this version of the events, "neither in mind, nor by raising or flinching his limbs, was he seen to struggle against his death".

The words of his self-commending are also significant, for Dionysius was the Ancient God of Fertility, His rites orgiastic, ending in the sacrifice of the male victim so that his blood could bring life to the earth. True, he might just have meant Dionysius the Areopagite, the assumed name of an otherwise anonymous sixth-century Mystical writer – though that seems highly unlikely. T. S. Eliot, writing the speech for *Murder in the Cathedral,* fastidiously side-steps the issue by changing Dionysius into "St Denys" – only slightly more likely than the mysterious Areopagite.

The final cryptic words were spoken by the knights: "He wished to be king, he wished to be more than king, let him be king".

*   *   *

Of course, it's the various traditional stories which form the basis of most subsequent legends – though one is backed by the apparently eye-witness account of a monk, Edward Grim, who claimed that he nearly had his arm cut off in the "struggle". It's too well-known to need much telling: the clash between Church and Crown, the "wicked" knights "aflame with terrible fury", composed speeches by Thomas which T. S. Eliot could have used unaltered, and the final "wounding of the sacrificial Lamb of God in the head . . ."

Another account, written by the chronicler, William Fitzstephen, though differing in many details, rises to genuine horror: "The holy archbishop received in all four strokes, all of them on the head, and the whole crown of the head was cut off . . . Then one of the murderers planted his foot on the neck of the holy martyr, as he lay dead, and cut with his sword's point the blood and brain from the cavity of the severed crown".

*   *   *

But, Saint or Sinner, Ritual Pagan Sacrifice or Holy Martyr, Thomas died . . . and, as on so many times before, the prudent collection of relics started immediately.

"While the body lay still on the pavement", wrote Brother Benedict, who had been "nearby" at the time, "some of the townsfolk of Canterbury . . . brought bottles and carried off secretly as much of the blood as they could. Others cut shreds of clothing and dipped them into the blood . . . ." Which might well have been intended for use during those fertility ceremonies, with the "townsfolk of Canterbury" knowing more of the truth *then* than we do *now*, and waiting for the chance. However, "some of the blood left over was carefully and cleanly collected" by the monks, "and poured into a clean vessel to be treasured up in the church" – along with "splinters of the sword which struck him down".

There are the usual disgusting details of that strange love they had for filth: "When his monks stripped his body for burial they found him wearing drawers and a shirt both made of harsh knotted haircloth, and swarming with vermin". Indeed, wrote one witness, "so infected with worms were they that anyone would judge the martyrdom light in comparison to wearing them". These "garments were at once put on view" in demonstration of his "heroic sanctity" . . . and, as though further proof were needed, his body bore the "severe lacerations" of recent scourgings.

"See, see," they cried, "how true a monk he was, and we knew it not".

And the miracles started that night: a man smeared his paralysed wife with a scrap of cloth soaked in the blood, and she was cured . . . and there were twenty more in the first three weeks. A year later the pilgrims were "flocking to the crypt" and "touching the coffin through the two holes" which the monks "had made for this purpose when they built the tomb around it" . . . with thousands of miracles reported, mostly cures – and two monks employed "all their time in recording them".

There was soon a brisk export business in the "profitable legacy" of that "cleanly collected" blood, as phials of "Canterbury Water" were distributed all over Europe . . . being water "to which", says Marc Alexander, "drops of his blood had been added, continually diluted to meet the ever-growing demand".

Not that *his* body was the only attraction, because the cathedral also possessed the complete bodies of St Alphege, St Anselm, and St Dunstan, with the "heads of three other Saints and the arms of eleven more", a piece of the True Cross, a thorn from the Holy Crown, wool woven by the Blessed Virgin Mary, a leg from Christ's cradle, Aaron's Rod, and "some of the clay out of which God made Adam".

Anyway, three years after his death, Thomas was canonised . . . and his body eventually had to be moved from the crypt to a new chapel behind the High Altar to make room for the vast crowds of pilgrims.

"Lo, surs", was the common cry all over England, "what vertu is it to call on Saynt Thomas in any tribulacion!"

Again, there were all the usual "mortifications of the body", with people walking barefoot, or shuffling along on their knees, and paying the attendant monks to flog them as "penance for their sins".

And his Shrine became the "glittering focal point of the whole cathedral".

Even the sensible Erasmus was impressed: "Every part glistened and shone and sparkled with rare and very large jewels, some of them bigger than a goose's egg".

And a Venetian described it more specifically: "It surpasses all belief, for, notwithstanding the great size, it is entirely covered over with plates of pure gold, though the gold is scarcely visible from the variety of precious stones with which it is studded . . . as diamonds, emeralds, sapphires . . . But everything is left behind by a ruby given by the King of France".

"The greatest concentration of portable wealth in England", says Marc Alexander.

At the Protestant Reformation it "took six or seven strong men to lift the two great chests in which its jewels and precious metals were packed to be transported to London" . . . and twenty-six carts for the other cathedral treasures.

"Tell me", said St Bernard, "what doth this gold in your sanctuary?"

Incidentally, Henry the Eighth had that great glowing ruby, the size of "an apricot", mounted on a thumb-ring for himself – as why wouldn't he? For wasn't he now the Defender of the Faith?

*   *   *

Such glory, such magnifience . . .

Gone, all gone . . . merely the inscription on the wall near the place where Thomas died . . . the mosaic floor where his Shrine stood, with that now familiar geometrical pattern of inter-acting circles and squares . . . and, much more moving, the worn stones of the famous Pilgrim's Steps leading to the Trinity

Chapel where the Shrine once stood, speaking so eloquently of the human misery and hope to which their slow erosion bears witness.

For those worn stones are worth more than all the gold and jewels on all the Shrines that ever were, or are, or ever will be: because faith, no matter how exploited by priests and hucksters, remains the Pearl of Great Price.

So please don't let your heart be troubled by the commercialism of the city, don't bother with the sort of "religious" trinkets which have been sold in and around the cathedral since pilgrimages began . . . but walk up those worn stone steps, and remember your Brothers and Sisters who have trodden them before you, perhaps kneel where they knelt, and believe whatsoever things are honest, just, pure, lovely, of good report. "If there be any virtue, and if there be any praise, think on these things".

*   *   *

Another popular English Shrine, second only to that of St Thomas, was up at Little Walsingham in Norfolk . . . though it began about a hundred years earlier, just before the Norman Conquest, and was already thriving during his lifetime. However, unlike most of the others, it was, according to Marc Alexander, "in a sense more mystical than the cult centres based on the physical remains of a recently deceased popular saint".

Seems that the Lady Richeldis de Favarques, the rich widow of the Lord of the local Manor, "prayed to Our Lady to tell her in what way She could best be honoured", and was "granted a Vision of the Blessed Virgin Mary", Who "took her in Spirit to Nazareth", and commanded her to build a replica of the "Holy House in which Jesus had lived as a Boy . . ."

Other versions of the legend say that it was actually the "house where the Annunciation had taken place", or the "house in which She had been born" . . . which, of course, could well have been one and the same.

Anyway, "two springs of water appeared where the Vision was seen", and that was proof enough for those (and other) days.

However, why this Cult of the Virgin should have started in Walsingham rather than Glastonbury has never been made clear. True, this part of North Norfolk is where the ancient power of the Mother Goddess was (and probably still is) very strong . . . and, says William Anderson, "a few miles to the south are the Neolithic flint-mines of Grimes Graves, where archeologists have found a propitiatory shrine on which the Goddess, carved in chalk as a heavily pregnant woman, was surrounded by antler picks". And the whole of Norfolk remains a "secret" country, a place where the "dark currents" flow with their often chilling strangeness.

There were several such Holy Houses in Medieval Europe, the most famous being enshrined in the Basilica at Loreto, near Ancona in Italy, which was claimed to be the "actual house" itself . . . first "transplanted by the hands of Angels" from Nazareth to a site between Fiume and Tersato on the Dalmatian Coast. Then, three years later, the "Angels came again by night and moved it to a wood near Recanati", and, later that year, they "moved it again to its present site" . . . there being little apparent reason for this Angelic restlessness.

And the innocent faithful of the Middle Ages believed . . . and so did Cardinal Newman and St Thérèse of Lisieux – and the Vatican has appointed Our Lady of Loreto as the "Patron of aviators" . . . so the idea retains obvious attractions.

Well, the Lady Richeldis was given measurements and minute directions for this replica at Walsingham, a wooden hut was built (which was significantly smaller than the stone house at Loreto), the Virgin Mary ("aided by Angelic Ministers") then moved it "two hundred fote and more in dystance" to its "proper" place . . . and the pilgrims started arriving, encouraged to believe that it was the real thing – that *this* was "England's Nazareth".

The original hut was eventually surrounded by a thatched building of stone and flint, then there was a large eleventh-century Priory for the Canons Regular of St Augustine who were the "Guardians of the Holy House", and then another Priory was built in the thirteenth century from which the Franciscans provided hospitality to the pilgrims . . . and, like all Shrines, the place possessed many valuable relics: a piece of the True Cross, some of the Virgin Mary's Milk, and a finger of St Peter – which could be "kissed for a fee".

There was also a wooden statue of the Blessed Virgin Mary seated with the Child Jesus on Her lap . . . with signs and wonders following: "Many seke ben here cured, Lame made hole and Blynde restored to syghte, Dede agayne revyved . . ." And also "lepers here recovered have be . . ."

Erasmus, that gentle and humane scholar, visited the Shrine at the beginning of the sixteenth century, said that "all things" were "bright with gold, silver, and precious stones" – but described the crystal phial of "Mary's Milk" as being "congealed" and reminding him of a "mixture of chalk and white of egg".

And there was all the usual commercial exploitation associated with holy places, now as well as then: "No less than seventeen inns catered for the needs of the Pilgrims, but the inn-keepers earned an evil reputation by scandalously overcharging. They looked upon the Shrine simply as a means of filling their own pockets".

Not that the inn-keepers were the only sinners, because the Augustinian Canons "looked upon their Shrine as a source of income", their Prior "led a scandalous life", and "dealt at his own will with the money and jewels there received".

Innocent faith and greed, alas, are never far apart: holiness and its exploitation seem joined at the roots.

*　　*　　*

It was all destroyed and looted during the Protestant Reformation of the sixteenth century, the statue of Our Lady of Walsingham taken to Smithfield and burned, and forgotten – except by the faithful few . . . but restored on a different site at the beginning of this century by an enthusiastic Anglo-Catholic Vicar, Father Hope-Patten, with that romantic view of Merry England popularised by G. K. Chesterton and Hillaire Belloc.

And now there are two Shrines, neither on the presumed site of the original: the Anglo-Catholic church in the village, and the Roman Catholic National Shrine of Our Lady about a mile out in the country – though there's a great deal of Ecumenical co-operation between them, especially shared Pilgrimages by coach from various parts of the country.

In the small Angol-Catholic church there's an enclosed chapel, the same measurements of the Holy House at Loreto, but made of brick and plaster – the "heart and centre" of which is a modern version of that original wooden statue of the Blessed Virgin Mary holding the Child Jesus, imaginatively reconstructed from a surviving souvenir badge sold to pilgrims during the high days of glory. This statue, based upon the flat image on the badge, is surprisingly tiny, and has the Virgin Mary wearing a large crown of jewel-encrusted gold and arrayed like a doll in gorgeous embroidered vestments, sitting on a high-backed throne, holding a lily as a foliated sceptre in Her right hand, and the Child Jesus on Her left knee. There's also another crown for use on various ceremonial occasions, and a wardrobe of other equally gorgeous dresses.

Close by, in the Sanctuary, there are "three fragments of the True Cross and other Relics for Veneration" ... and that Holy Well, the water of which you may drink as "an aid to Spiritual Healing", is just round the corner at the foot of some marble steps. Though it's admitted that this Well is not the original one used in the Middle Ages, the belief is that the water may possibly come from the same source ... and "three dowsers have traced it" in that general direction.

The Roman Catholic Shrine is a large and impressive contemporary wooden church, with a small separate chapel, converted from the Saxon barn at which Medieval Pilgrims coming up the "Way of Milk" from London were supposed to have removed their shoes and made their confessions before walking bare-footed into the shrine at Walsingham – hence its present name, Slipper Chapel. In it there's a wooden copy of the Anglo-Catholic statue, though more austere, lacking the vestments.

The village is sixteenth-century, picture-postcard, and commercially geared to the wants of Pilgrims and tourists: tea, coffee, beer, fizzy drinks, fish-and-chips, books, pamphlets, religious trinkets ...

And yet ... and yet ...

For how very much like our own times were those distant high days of Walsingham: wars and rumours of wars, starvation and disease in the world and corruption "in the seats of the mighty", violence on the streets, uncertainty. The Pilgrims went there because they desperately wanted peace, consolation, a reminder that there *was* another world than this ... and there are worse things to want, surely.

Yes, they were exploited, often defrauded, even deluded in some of their beliefs ... but the Norfolk countryside has a clear light and serene beauty all its own, and we could do ourselves a lot of innocent good to walk our own way around, think our own thoughts about our own "pilgrimage through Time to Eternity", and remember that governments needn't always have the last word, that television isn't everything – and that if the Word was truly "made flesh, and dwelt among us", then He had to live *somewhere*, Boy and Man, with *any* house becoming a home

161

when Love is the fire.

The old anonymous Walsingham poem says much the same:
"For true love is a durable fire,
In the mind ever burning,
Never sick, never old, never dead,
From itself never turning".

*   *   *

Twenty years after the Lady Richeldis had that wooden hut built at Walsingham, with the fame of it already spreading through East Anglia, Bishop Walkelin was ordering the start of the Norman Cathedral at Winchester in Hampshire . . . and them now going up all over the country: Canterbury, Chichester, Durham, Ely, Gloucester, Lincoln, Norwich, Ripon, York . . .

"It was as if the whole earth were clothing itself anew in a white robe of churches", wrote a contemporary monk . . . and the hammers of the masons were loud in the land.

Winchester had been the capital of England for two-hundred-and-fifty years, and, it says here, "the city's successive cathedrals bear witness to its importance". Pages of history, the gildings of legend: Wessex, the Saxons, St Swithun and his Forty Days of Rain, King Alfred, Willaim Rufus buried in a marble tomb beneath the central tower . . .

Interesting story about that: Seems that the tower fell down when he was first buried there, because, according to popular belief, he was "an heretical king to be allowed hallowed ground". And it's true that he was "interred with indecent haste, not a prayer was said for the repose of his soul" . . . and the "complete lack of ceremonial for an annointed sovereign's funeral suggests that there was more to it than dislike". So the ordinary people obviously knew more about the facts of his "sacrificial" death in the New Forest than their clerical historians were willing to put into writing.

Anyway, the tower was rebuilt, and he's still there, along with assorted bishops and various of the nobility . . . though Isaac Walton rests there on the banks of a gentle stream in Paradise, and Jane Austen is making mental notes on the daily comedy of manners. And King Arthur's Round Table is hanging on the wall somewhere or other . . .

But the holiest ground in Winchester Cathedral is a yard or two of "thirteenth-century encaustic tiles" on the floor of the "retrochoir" ... which, being translated, means an area of decorated fired-tiles on the floor behind the Choir.

At casual glance not much to see: square, reddish-brown, simple patterns, circles, triangles, leaves ... but they were made by the hands of ordinary men whose names have not survived, who dug the clay, worked and shaped it, drew the designs – perhaps with the help and skill of their wives and daughters ... and who then fired and glazed and fired again, and set them where they have stayed to this walking day.

Ordinary men and women, who would have "makyn" Pilgrimage along the Old Road to Canterbury, perhaps up to Walsingham, "working and wandering as the world demanded", who were often hungry and more often cold, who lived in hovels, were sick, diseased, even despised ...

"Sum good, my gentyll mayster", was the cry of the lepers and beggers on their streets, "sum good for God's sake".

Who died for the ambitions and quarrels of their kings, were exploited by their "lords and masters", persuaded to believe in legends and frauds by their bishops and priests.

Yet these people laid those tiles, raised high those roof-beams, carved and sawed and hammered, cut and coloured that stained-glass, heaved and pulled and laboured ...

The kings have their grand tombs, the bishops have their "peach-blossom marble", the nobles have their flattering inscriptions ... but if you seek a monument to a "fair field of folk", please look at those tiles.

* * *

And it wasn't only the cathedrals being built in the cities, churches in the towns and villages, but the great monastic abbeys in remote places, to which the monks retreated as an "escape from the snares of the world, the flesh, and the Devil".

To us their "retreats" are beautiful, often romantic valleys with the high mountains for a backdrop – but to the Middle Ages they were deserts, hostile to life, roaming with wolves, lairs of darkness and terror.

For instance, in the twelfth century, about forty years after the completion of the Norman Cathedral at Winchester, thirteen monks of a rich monastery at York grew dissatisfied with the "corrupt and indulgent" life of their Brethren under the dispensation of the "elderly and kindly Abbot", and "did most earnestly beseech" the Archbishop to "grant unto them land whereon they could build an house" in which they could live more in "harmony with their Rule". And, according to Brother Serlo, one of those beseechers, they were granted "a place remote and uninhabited, set with thorns, amongst the hollows of the mountains and rocks, more fit, it seemed, for the dens of wild beasts than for human use".

With a slightly later chronicler agreeing: a site of "horror and vast solitude in a deep and gloomy valley about three miles from Ripon, where they began in extreme poverty to build a church" . . . which grew over the next four hundred years into one of the most magnificent of all Cistercian Monasteries: Fountains Abbey, in Skeldale.

True, it was looted and destroyed during the Protestant Reformation, but even the present ruins are awe-inspiring. They stand in acres and acres of parkland, there are lakes and ornamental ponds and cascades, trees, walks, formal gardens . . . and you leave your car, stroll down the bank, in through wrought-iron gates (where, inevitably, you pay), on along a mile or so of winding paths between those trees and that life-giving water, turn another corner, and *there* they are: grey stones, crumbling walls, arches, pillars, towers, spires, buttresses . . . everything strangely familiar . . .

"I have been here before . . ."

Stones to be seen which have long since crumbled, fallen . . . your eyes follow the lines of vanished curves . . . expect a fan of vaulting, and see the vault of Heaven . . . listen for you hardly know what, and hear peace, the presence of mystery. Grasses and wildflowers grow from the cracks and crevices, birds roost where the statues of kings and queens and saints and prophets once stood, and there's that feeling of history, time past . . . men have lived here, broken bread, walked these cloistered pavements, chanted the Praises of God, been sad or happy, died, passed on to wherever . . .

And *this* is all that's left: stones, echoing stones.

Fountains, Rievaulx below the Moors of North Yorkshire, Tintern beside the River Wye in Gwent . . . these three, all movingly beautiful, even in their desolation, "bare ruined choirs where late the sweet birds sang . . ."

So why not listen to that singing?

Go to any or all, choose a day or a time when there aren't many other people about, a Monday, or a late afternoon, or the weather a drizzle of fine rain, and stand near where the High Altar once stood . . . and hear those voices coming to you from the silence on the other side of time . . .

Quietly, quietly . . . rising, chanting the Hour of the Divine Office, the Latin words mysterious, the music sensuous, remote, reaching you from further than mere distance, plaintive, whispering of private misery and hard-won peace, telling of joy and loneliness and sorrow and exultation, praising, praying, pleading . . .

And hear echoes from the wilderness of the early Church, see those who fled into the deserts from the wickedness of their world, the hermits and anchorites, solitaries in their meditations . . . and then remember those congregations of monks in that very place, singing these songs, chanting the same words all those hundreds of years ago, day after day, filling their lives with what they knew as Glory . . .

Yes, there was corruption . . . but, surely, some of our dead Brothers were also standing on Holy Ground.

*　　*　　*

And there are many such places which aren't in ruins, which survive, changed, enlarged, restored, renovated . . . but which, if seen and experienced with the eyes and faith of a child or pilgrim, can still move your imagination with all their magnificence.

Chichester Cathedral in West Sussex, Durham where Cuthbert has now found his rest – with one last and lovely thought about Himself . . .

Those robes he was found in when they examined him at the beginning of this century – they were of silk, embroidered with seals, fishes, and eider ducks . . . for even in death he has not been divided from his friends, the wild creatures.

Then there's Gloucester . . .

*   *   *

Some lovely things in Gloucester Cathedral, where once the round piers of the nave were "painted with patterns of vegetation in vivid greens and yellows" . . . No, we are never far from those groves . . .

And there's that great fretted tower, the Lady Chapel, the marvellous fan-vaulting in the Cloisters . . . but walk on beneath the branches of that vaulting, remember the trees of the forest, and go on until you come to the Lavatorium, the place where the Benedictine monks "performed their ablutions" . . . washed . . .

Now, as we've seen, few of the Saints and not all of the monks were good friends with the "Sister Water" of St Francis, who wasn't exactly besotted himself . . . but there's a most human and even humorous touch above each of the stalls along the stone-trough: small stained-glass windows depicting the use of water in the Bible. Jesus washing the feet of St Peter, or walking on the waves of Galilee, or commanding the storm to be still, or turning the water into wine at the Marriage Feast of Cana . . . and there's the Angel "stirring" the Pool of Bethesda, the woman "offering Jesus wherewith to drink" at the well, the miraculous "draught of fishes" . . . even Noah riding out the Flood . . .

But, apart from St Peter's reluctant feet, there's no actual washing!

Yet, to stand where our Brothers stood is to remember their humanity, to be at one with them . . . even reconciled to their ways.

*　　*　　*

Or Lincoln Cathedral, which John Ruskin regarded as "out and out the most precious piece of architecture in the British Isles". And even D. H. Lawrence, no lover of orthodox Christianity, was passionately intense about its beauty.

"When he saw the cathedral in the distance, dark blue lifted watchfully in the sky, his heart leapt. It was the sign in heaven, it was the Spirit hovering like a dove, like an eagle over the earth".

Then he pushed open the door, "and the great, pillared gloom was before him, in which his soul shuddered and rose from her nest. His soul leapt, soared up into the great church. His body stood still, absorbed by the height. His soul leapt up into the gloom, into possession, it reeled, it swooned with a great escape, it quivered in the womb, in the hush and gloom of fecundity, like seed of procreation in ecstasy".

Which would doubtless have shocked St Hugh, the man "central to the whole history and life of the place", and whose "bodily austerities" were famous even in his own flesh-mortifying day . . . but at least Lawrence is responding to beauty with everything he's got: a man rarely in good health, a Mystic in whom life burned until it killed him, *knowing* wholeness when he saw it, exulting in holiness . . .

"Away from time, always outside of time! Between east and

west, between dawn and sunset, the church lay like a seed in silence, dark before germination, silenced after death. Containing birth and death, potential with all the noise and transition of life, the cathedral remained hushed, a great, involved seed, whereof the flower would be radiant life inconceivable, but whose beginning and whose end were the circle of silence. Spanned round with the rainbow, the jewelled gloom folded music upon silence, light upon darkness, fecundity upon death as a seed folds leaf upon leaf and silence upon the root and the flower, hushing up the secret of all between its parts, the death out of which it fell, the life into which it has dropped, the immortality it involves, and the death it will embrace again".

All you have to do is push open that door.

★   ★   ★

And then there's Wells, close to the Mendip Hills, not far from Glastonbury in Somerset . . . but as different as any two such places could be: one all ruins and legends, the other neat and tidy and domestic . . . one moody, the other gently magnificent.

"The town, cathedral, and bishop's palace", it says here, "form a harmonious whole, closely integrated and yet clearly separate one from the other".

And there are all the usual words, bits and bobs of information, names, dates, facts and figures . . .

The place has been holy since the ceremonial days of Stonehenge and earlier, with the very name "Wells" telling of Sacred Springs and the blessings of the Great Mother. There's an ancient tomb-chamber with fragments of painted wall-plaster, the Romans built round some of those springs, the first wooden and thatched church was ordered by the King of Wessex at the end of the seventh century, the Saxons replaced wood with flint . . . and by the eleventh century there was "a large and imposing stone cathedral". Then the Normans . . . then a "new Early English style building on a fresh site a few yards to the North . . ."

And then the Protestant Reformation . . .

But it's a truly beautiful holy place, inside and out.

For instance, the West Front, all honey-coloured stone, is the "largest gallery of Medieval sculpture in the world", Apostles, Prophets, Martyrs, Saints, Popes, Kings, Queens, Bishops, Knights in armour, Priests . . . though please spare a thought for that "fair field full of folk" who did all the actual work.

And there are some lovely monuments elsewhere . . .

A staircase of shallow steps up to the Chapter House, broad under the high arches, worn into the same sorts of hollows as those at Canterbury, still speaking of the generations which "have trod, have trod, have trod . . ." Yes, it's a slow cascade of stone held in time, a moment in and out of eternity . . .

And the Chapter House at the top is another Southwell, another octagonal grove of Sacred Trees, slightly less obviously Pagan, but springing with surrounding saplings of Purbeck marble, a great central trunk vaulting and fanning into over-arching branches and clusters of leaves and flowers . . . light filtering into the glade through the traceried glass . . .

So hear the deepest secret of silence there in the High Places of Her Hill, for She sings a song that is never done: "Now is my Love's Holy Day", wrote John Rowlands Pritchard there. "The drum beats early and late".

*   *   *

And then there's the famous fourteenth-century clock, similar to the one Peter Lightfoot made for Glastonbury Abbey: that squared-circle symbolising the New Jerusalem, with the Angels holding the Four Winds, the Sun, the Earth, and the Moving Moon in Her Mysteries, the Microcosm and Macrocsm, humanity as the image of the Universe . . .

Yes, join the crowds who gather on the hour with their cameras to take photographs of the toy horsemen who joust and flail around on top as the bell clanks the time, good fun for the children – though one of the two riders dies in the mechanical journey, and even the death of a toy is an unnecessary sadness . . . but stay afterwards, spend some time with time.

Because the whole idea of natural time is passing from our world: the rising and setting of the sun, the phases of the moon, Her waxing and waning, the seasons swelling to fruitfulness, life and death and resurrection . . . all these are almost things of the past. For we think to measure time in numbers not movements,

169

by digital flickerings not the circular sweep of stars and planets across the face of the Heavens. The instantaneous print-out will soon replace clocks and dials and minute-hands with split-second data-observations twitching away our days . . . leaving such quaintness to cathedrals and other museums for the "remembrance of things past . . ."

Man is now the one who measures, not who is measured.

*   *   *

Beneath this clock there's a modern shrouded figure of the Risen Christ, carved from a yew-tree, that ancient wood of death and the tomb, His arms still outstretched in the rigidity of crucifixion . . .

But Risen! Halleluiah! Risen!

For the strips of grave-cloth are falling away from His Body . . .

Yes, His hands and feet and Sacred Head are still sore-wounded, Heart still aching with what *we* did to our Suffering Servant . . .

But soon He will meet His Beloved Mary Magdalene, soon be having His breakfast of broiled fish on the shores of Galilee . . . be meeting His friends who fled at His arrest . . . forgiving them . . .

Be Ascending . . .

"The, er, Resurrection?" say some of our bishops. "Well, yes, there's some, er, extremely exciting theology in the pipe-line, new understandings of existential concepts . . ."

So spend some time with this Christ . . .

He may not be with us in *quite* such a human form for very much longer.

How can you carve a statue of an "existential concept"?

*   *   *

Somewhere along those pavements of Wells Cathedral, between that Chapter House and the Lady Chapel, easy to miss in the cool grey twilight, there's a tomb, one among many: my Brother Giso, bishop of the place from 1061 to 1088, a monk from Lorraine, chaplain in his time to Edward the Confessor.

Nothing much to see, only the reclining effigy in marble or alabaster, coped and mitred, the face and praying hands of the dead worn smooth with the touch of innumerable living hands . . .

Well, when I was walking by on my self-important way to elsewhere I was strangely disturbed, and felt that I had to stop, had to know who this man was. And I stood there, looked down into what was left of his face, folded my hands around his . . . and somehow experienced his pain, *knew* that he had suffered – but was now at rest.

Two minutes, five minutes . . . how long is time at a time like that?

And then, even more strangely reluctant, I left him in sculptured death, and walked on my way to wherever.

My wife later discovered that his tomb had recently been opened in the cause of archeology, and they'd found his poor bones . . . with eight of the vertebrae from the base of his spine fused together in the daily agony of osteo-arthritis.

I also have suffered and still occasionally suffer from osteo-arthritis . . . and so know his pain to this mortal day.

Yes, he called across nine hundred years . . . and I'm glad I heard.

Sleep, my Brother Giso . . . take your rest.

171

The Recluse atte Norwych

Three hundred years after the Lady Richeldis had that Vision of Our Lady up at Walsingham, there was another woman of Norfolk having quite another sort of Vision: the Lady Julian, a fourteenth-century Mystic, who also knew about love.

"Wouldest thou wit thy Lord's meaning?" she says. "Wit it well: Love was His meaning".

Yes, dear Julian of Norwich, who lived most of her life as an Anchoress walled up in a room the size of a small kitchen . . . with an Anchoress being a woman Hermit, one who renounces the world to live in the seclusion of a cell or anchorhold, especially for religious reasons. Both words are steeped in the history of the early Church: hermit, from the Greek *eremites,* dweller in the desert . . . and the Greek *anchoreo,* I withdraw. Some of those who "withdrew" did so into the literal desert or remote place – but some "withdrew from society" into a hut or cell attached to a church . . . where, according to Michael McLean, their "anchored presence amid the community was seen as a challenge to the activism of ordinary people and a symbol of stability in faith".

Well, her one short book, *Revelations of Divine Love,* the first known book by an English woman, is now regarded as one of the great classics of the Spiritual Life, and many people believe that the way of Julian is the best way through our contemporary Dark Wood, "where the straight road is wholly lost and gone".

As we have seen with St Cuthbert and St Guthlac, the Vocation for a solitary life of prayer and contemplation was common enough in the Middle Ages – though Julian was obviously far more balanced than poor Guthlac.

True, nothing very much is know for certain about her, except her Christian name – and even that may merely have been traditionally associated with her because her cell was probably against the wall of a church dedicated to St Julian the Hospitaller. But, from what she tells us in her book, at the age of thirty, after a desperate illness, she had a Vision of the Head of Christ, bleeding beneath the Crown of Thorns, and then sixteen "shewynges" or revelations . . . and later wrote (or probably dictated) her book about them.

She then lived the rest of her days as a recluse, with only a necessary rat-catching cat for company, entombed in the symbolic grave of that cell. Yes, there was a servant who lived outside, and cooked the simple food, and there was a little window (probably shuttered on the inside) looking on the street, to which pilgrims came in search of spiritual counsel – so she was not an absolute and total solitary. But she spent thirty or forty or perhaps even fifty years on her own in that cell, remembering her "shewynges" . . . "dead unto the world and alive unto God" . . . meditating on their meaning: Love . . . "the marvellous music of unending Love . . ."

Hardly the sort of life to inspire any normal man or woman of the twentieth century.

And yet . . . and yet . . .

★   ★   ★

"The only thing that can save the world from complete moral collapse", wrote Thomas Merton, "is a spiritual revolution . . . and the desire for unworldliness, detachment, and Union with God is the most fundamental expression of this revolutionary spirit".

Well, yes, agreed: he *was* an Enclosed Contemplative Monk at the time, and a Trappist at that, vowed to Obedience, Poverty, Chastity, and Silence – so he could be unsympathetically likened to the Fox finding virtue in the loss of his own tail.

Except that he then goes on: "It is certainly not possible, nor even desirable, that every Christian should leave the world and enter a Trappist monastery".

So all he meant was that, as ever and always, "the world is too much with us", that "we lay waste our powers", and "have given our hearts away . . ." Amen, Brother Thomas.

★   ★   ★

I live on the North Norfolk Coast about twenty or so miles from Norwich, and often remember Julian, occasionally visit her cell there.

No, not that it's your actual genuine undamaged and intact

174

holy place: six hundred years of time and chance and neglect and war have worn away and broken down the mere wood and stones.

There was probably a wooden Saxon church on the site, but the Danes destroyed the area at the beginning of the eleventh century, and, says the guide-book, "nothing of the early work can certainly be traced".

During the reign of King Canute it was rebuilt in flint, "a little thatched building on open land", various bits and pieces were added as and when and wherever, time passed, there were years of wind and weather and the doings of other kings and many priests ... until, by the late eighteenth century, the building was "in a sorry state", there weren't any Services being held ... and then, one "Monday morning" in 1845, "at about eight o'clock, the end of the Chancel fell in", the "great noise alarmed the neighbours", and there was a "proposal to demolish".

But, somehow, it survived, and was restored and tinkered with, new stones added, maintained ... until, during the Second World War, a German bomb reduced it to rubble.

However, says the guide-book, "the growing awareness of the importance of the Lady Julian's writings caused yet another restoration".

★   ★   ★

And there it now stands, a pleasant little church, only a very short walk up the hill to the centre of Norwich, with a small Chapel on what is more than likely the site of her cell: indeed, "there are two pieces of flintwork near the ground" which are believed to have "formed part of the early foundations". In other words, it's an imaginative reconstruction . . . and Pilgrims come from all over the world to pray in this place.

And, as the cars and lorries surge by outside, as the motor-bikes thunder, it's difficult not to agree that Julian and Thomas Merton were onto something – because there's an interior silence, an air of peace, the centainty that there's another time than the anxious present, another world than the one making so much useless noise. It's a reminder that even in the lovely depths of rural East Anglia this "harsh and dense" Dark Wood we wander through can still be the way down into the "chambers of Hell", that there's sometimes more "getting and spending" in the decent little city of Norwich than is possible for a good conscience. Life is "seared with trade, bleared, smeared with toil", there's national and international lunacy . . . "the ceremony of innocence is drowned . . ."

So, yes, there's a lot to be said for Julian, who lived in an equally fearful world: the Black Death, the Hundred Years War, the Revolt of the Peasants . . . and who "withdrew" from it in search of "unworldliness, detachment" . . . even "Union with God . . ."

Yet she was never so Heavenly-minded as to be no earthly use, because her thought is always sensible and practical: We have a responsibility to love ourselves as well as our fellow human-beings, for, she wrote, "all men are as one man, because one Man was as all men".

Or, as we would put it in these less sexist days, "all people are as one person, because one Person was as all people".

Yet she also described God with the "fair lovely word *Mother*", so was obviously far less sexist than many of our contemporary theologians who insist on the "maleness" of their Deity.

But Love is always her answer: Yes, we can transmit coloured television pictures around the world and back, we can travel two or three times faster than sound, could destroy the earth and all who live on it at the touch of a few red buttons . . . but do we love ourselves or each other?

If we *did*, would there be any of those red buttons?

*　　*　　*

"I beg you all for God's sake", she wrote, "and advise you for your own, to stop thinking about the poor wretch who was shewn these things".

So there's no need to stay long, to lock the door and throw away the key as she did . . . but ten minutes, half-an-hour on your own in peace and quietness . . . and then, in her own haunting words, "All shall be well, and all shall be well, and all manner of thing shall be well".

Whispers of Immortality

And then, eventually, the Protestant Reformation, the attempted replacing of works by Faith, deeds by the Word, the image by the text, the High Altar by the higher pulpit.

The hammers and the crowbars, the thumbscrews and the rack, the fires, the block, the gallows and the disembowelling knife . . . the Tower, Tyburn, Smithfield . . . King Henry the Eighth, the two Bloody Queens, bishops . . .

Heroism, yes . . . the blood and ashes of the Holy Martyrs, Roman Catholic and Protestant, Brothers and Sisters in the One Christ.

When they burned the pregnant Perotine Massey alive she gave birth at the stake, and they threw the baby into the flames with her.

Was *she* Roman Catholic or Protestant?

Were *they* Protestant or Roman Catholic?

Does it matter?

But where, except at that stake, was there any holy ground?

Please forgive us, Perotine Massey.

*   *   *

John Donne, Dean of Old St Paul's Cathedral, was "much possessed by death", and often preached on his own holy ground. And his most famous sermon, *Death's Duel*, was delivered by him, "before the King's Majesty", Charles, on the Dean's "customary day", the First Friday in Lent, 1630, not many days before his death, "as if, having done this, there remained nothing for him to do but die".

He preached it when "his sickness had left him but so much flesh as did only cover his bones", and when he "appeared in the pulpit many of the beholders thought he presented himself not to preach mortification by a living voice, but mortality by a decayed body, and a dying face".

Full of haunting images: "We have a winding-sheet in our mother's womb which grows with us from our conception, and we come into the world wound up in that winding-sheet, for we come to seek a grave''.

Intense with terrible disgust: "But then is death the end of all? Is that dissolution of body and soul the last death that the body shall suffer? It is not, though this be the exit from life: it is the entrance into the death of corruption and putrefaction, and vermiculation, and incineration, and dispersion in and from the grave, in which every dead man dies over again . . . this death after death, nay, this death after burial, this dissolution after dissolution . . ."

Crawling with channering worms: "We must all say with Job, *Corruption, thou art my father, and to the worm, Thou art my mother and my sister* . . . My mouth shall be filled with dust, and the *worm shall feed, and feed sweetly upon me,* for we all *lie down alike in the dust, and the worm covers* us . . ."

Passionate with the Passion of His Christ: "There now hangs that Sacred Body upon the Cross, rebaptised in His own Tears, and Sweat, and enbalmed in His own Blood alive. There are those bowels of compassion which are so manifested, as that you may see them through His wounds. There are those glorious eyes grew faint in their sight . . ."

And yet urgent with the Promise of the Easter Sunday Morning to come after this First Friday of Lent: "There I leave you in that Blessed Dependency, to hang upon Him that hangs upon the Cross, there bathe in His tears . . . and lie down in peace in His grave, till He vouchsafe you a Resurrection, and an Ascension into that Kingdom which he hath prepared for you with the inestimable price of His incorruptible Blood. Amen".

No use going to St Pauls for a sermon the like of that *these* days, Lent or not.

★   ★   ★

And then the "recorder of his days", Isaac Walton, tells us what happened: "The next day after his sermon, his strength being much wasted . . . easily yielded at this very time to have a monument made. Without delay a choice painter was got to be in readiness to draw his picture, which was taken as followeth. Several charcoal fires being first made in his large study, he brought with him into that place his winding-sheet in his hand, and having put off all his clothes, had this sheet put on him, and so tied with knots at his head and feet, and his hands so placed as dead bodies are usually fitted, to be shrouded and put into their coffin, or grave. He thus stood, with his eyes shut, and with so much of the sheet turned aside as might shew his lean, pale, and death-like face, which was purposely turned towards the East, from whence he expected the Second Coming of his and our Saviour Jesus. In this posture he was drawn at his just height, and when the picture was fully finished, he caused it to be set by his bedside, where it continued and became his hourly object till his death . . ."

Which was not long . . . "He closed his own eyes, and then disposed his hands and body into such a posture, as required not the least alteration by those who came to shroud him".

His friends "caused his shrouded likeness" to be taken from

the picture and "thus carved in one entire piece of white marble", as it "now stands in that Church . . ."
Well, "that Church" was destroyed in the Great Fire of London . . . but his monument survived, though seared by those purgatorial flames, and there he is, on the right-hand side of the south choir-aisle as you walk up towards the Lady Chapel, his eyes closed, waiting for those Angels to blow their trumpets at "the round earth's imagin'd corners", so that he can "arise from death" and to his "scatter'd body go".

*   *   *

All the rest of St Pauls is overwhelming architecture, that famous Dome, the Glories of our Blood and State: "Since the marriage of the Prince of Wales and Princess Diana", announces the Official Guide, "it has become one of the most-visited of all our major churches".

The buses and coaches at the kerb, boots and shoes across the pavements and up the steps, in and along and around, over the tiles and the slabs and the names of the Mighty Dead . . .

"The Church of the Nativity in Bethlehem has so far been my worst example of cross commercialism", says Harold Jackson of *The Guardian*. "Pandemonium . . . The religious connection is, at the very least, elusive".

Past Doctor Johnson in a Roman toga and all the other statues and busts and memorials, inscriptions, dates, voices, always the voices, around the far end, and back along . . . and then the gift-shop, cards, horse-brasses, full-colour transparencies, tin tea-caddies, tasteless trinkets . . . and out into the clear daylight and the waiting buses and coaches . . .

Voices, always voices . . . "footfalls echo in the memory" . . . and this bell, softly . . . a man kneeling . . .

For a Service? Choral Evensong? or what?

"If we understand aright the dignity of this bell that tolls for our Evening Prayer . . . it doth toll for him that thinks it doth . . . So never send to know for whom the bell tolls . . ."

It tolled for thee, John Donne . . . and now you know all about that "death after death, this dissolution after dissolution . . ."

Fed the worm sweetly upon you?

Yet you stand now on your own and holy ground, there being

182

"no penance due to innocence" . . . and your body, which was once "naked first", has "become a small quantity of Christian dust".

"But", says Friend Walton, "I shall see it re-animated".

In *that* Faith and Glorious Hope, then. Amen.

★   ★   ★

Thomas Traherne was seven years old when John Donne composed himself in death, and there was never a more gently child-like man.

"Certainly", he wrote in his *Centuries of Meditations*, "Adam in Paradise had not more sweet and curious apprehensions of the world, than when I was a child".

He was born in Hereford, was the Vicar of a little church near there for most of his life, died at the age of thirty-four, and remained a Holy Innocent all his days.

"The corn was orient and immortal wheat, which never should be reaped, nor was ever sown. I thought it had stood from everlasting to everlasting. The dust and the stones of the street were as precious as gold . . . the city seemed to stand in Eden, or to be built in Heaven . . ."

So, yes, the pulpit of that church at Credenhill, four or five miles out of Hereford, would by holy enough ground.

Indeed, with him and through his eyes, the "green trees" can "transport and ravish" you, their "sweetness and unusual beauty" can make your "heart to leap" . . . and "Eternity" can be "manifest in the Light of the Day . . ."

★   ★   ★

Or you can visit Little Gidding in Cambridgeshire, between Huntingdon and Oundle, about four mile west of the Great North Road – but difficult to find, even "from the place you would be likely to come from . . . taking any route, starting from anywhere . . ."

Though why would you want to be coming here at all?

There's the site of a Medieval village "which was deserted after the Black Death in the fourteenth century", a few ridges and depressions in the field "where the cottages stood and the peasants had their strips for cultivation" . . . and a small, a very small Chapel.

And, as T. S. Eliot wrote, "You are here to kneel where prayer has been valid".

Because Little Gidding is where Nicholas Ferrar founded his Community at the beginning of the seventeeth century: an attempt to "combine the values of monastic and family life" . . . which survives to this breathing day. "A life of simplicity", writes Margaret Drabble, "prayer and service, in a unique quiet blend of mysticism and practical, well-managed common sense".

Nicholas Ferrar was the son of a wealthy London merchant, was educated at Clare College in Cambridge, became Deputy Treasurer of the Virginia Company, served briefly as a Member of Parliament, was offered various "high posts in government" . . . but became convinced that his "ultimate vocation was Community Life in the quiet service of God", abandoned trade and politics, chose Little Gidding for its "remoteness and tranquility", settled here with thirty or so friends, renovated the ruined Manor house and derelict Medieval church – which was a "hay-barn and Hog-sty" . . . and died at the age of forty-five in 1637, the year Thomas Traherne was born.

The Community was always small, but they prayed together and worked hard, grew much of their own simple food, made plain furniture, bound books, wove tapestry, dispensed "potions and ointments to the sick", taught the local children to read and write, were hospitable to strangers . . . and loved one another.

And then, like many such Communities before and since, with deaths and sectarian bitterness, it died out. Stones and bricks crumbled, tiles slipped, old timber rotted, the weeds regained their green kingdom . . . two-hundred-and-fifty years of slow decay . . .

"Outside the circle of those interested in the byways of ecclesiastical history", wrote Helen Gardner, "Little Gidding was obscure and forgotten".

But in the twentieth century there has been a "growing movement among Christians towards the renewal of Community Life", and the "curiously modern" experiment of Nicholas Ferrar has "come to be recognised". And the "rebirth" of Little Gidding "has been part of this wider movement", with the poetry of T. S. Eliot's *Four Quartets* doing most to "encourage interest" in the revival of this "Spiritual powerhouse from which the Church and Her children may draw strength".

Eliot visited the Community on a "really lovely day" at the end of May in 1936, and the whole place "compelled" his "imagination many days, many days and many hours" . . . so that when he wrote the last of his *Four Quartets* during the Second World War the "experience" was waiting for his "meaning" to emerge: and he called the poem *Little Gidding* in acknowlegement. For, to quote Helen Gardner again, "he found a symbol of the irrelevance of victory or defeat to the Divine economy in this shrine of an obscure saint of the Church".

*   *   *

And there it all is, the poetry and the place, "beyond any meaning we can assign to happiness" . . . with the Community of Christ the Sower as real as the words: a few families, a few people, a few children . . . Anglican, Roman Catholic, Methodist . . . common worship, combining "quiet simplicity with a rich sacramental life", shared meals, five acres of land under cultivation, workshops . . .

"What the dead had no speech for, when living, they can tell you, being dead", wrote Eliot: "the communication of the dead is tongued with fire beyond the language of the living".

Again, not a lot to see: the small brick Chapel with the strangely ornate stone facade, an architrave above the door and a bell and Classical mouldings and a thin pyramid and a ball balanced on top and then a wee metal flag . . . and the panelled interior and barrelled roof and facing stalls, a brass Eagle lectern, some bits and pieces of donated this and that, a Victorian stained-glass Crucifixion all sentimental piety, chequered black and white stone floor . . . and a Gothic and gold exhortation above the Sanctuary:

O Pray for the peace of Jerusalem . . .

Yet an abiding sense that here is a "condition of complete simplicity", a timeless moment "suspended in time . . ."

The book for Visitors is eloquent with the names and addresses from the "round earth's imagin'd corners", in the graveyard there are roses and stone slabs and worn inscriptions, the weathered tomb of Nicholas Ferrar between the door and the landscape, great trees, those "blue remembered" distances . . . the knowledge that "History is now and England".

★   ★   ★

"I will not by the noise of bloody wars and the dethroning of kings advance you to glory", wrote Thomas Traherne, not long after the bloody Civil War and the dethroning and execution of a king: "but by the gentle ways of peace and love".

But the times, as always, were against the Thomas Trahernes of this world, and the "Gospel of the Spirit" was loud upon his "green fields and shining streets" . . . with the loudest of the proclaimers being the Ranters: so named because their enthusiastic preaching sounded like "mere ranting" to orthodox ears, "so much shouting of God as to deafen men". And the Ranters themselves claimed to be among the Brethren of the Free Spirit.

This was a religious movement which wild-fired across Europe during the previous century, with the Brethren (*and* Sisters) intent upon their own personal and individual Salvation, "extreme individualists who found reassurance in brotherhood". They indeed "thirsted after righteousness", but, in the opinion of their hostile clerical critics, tended to overstress the value of their apparently "ecstatic" experiences – and, unlike those within a living tradition of such Mysticism, they acknowledged "no authority at all save their own". Each small group was autonomous, with its own Leader, and having its own particular practices, rites, and articles of belief. Many claimed the "gifts of prophecy, healing, and of tongues" as promised to the Church in the New Testament. There were dozens of men and women all over the country claiming to be "Elijah" or "Christ", new "prophets" and "healers" on nearly every village green, "strange doctrines" in many pulpits.

The Ranters inherited this Free Spirit. Both during and after the confusions of the Civil War "religious excitement ran high", and many felt that "God was pouring out His Spirit upon all flesh". Ecstasy was an "everyday occurance", prophecies were "uttered in all directions", and "millennial hopes were rife throughout the population".

★   ★   ★

And the "loudest of these loud spouters of God" was George Fox, dear "old leather-breeches" himself – the "gatherer of a people called Quakers" . . . or *The Religious Society of Friends* as they prefer to be known today. True, he (and his Friends) regarded the Ranters as "erring souls to be converted" . . . but claimed that God "spoke" to him: indeed, his *Journal* is sometimes strident with such phrases as "the Lord's power broke forth", or "the Lord's power was so great that the house seemed to be shaken". And he was consequently lumped with the Ranters by most of his contemporaries.

He'd been "discontent with the shams" of his age and "pining after Spiritual Truth" for several years. "I fasted much", he wrote, "walked abroad in solitary places many days, and often took my Bible, and sat in hollow trees and lonesome places until night came on, and frequently in the night walked mournfully about by myself, for I was a man of sorrows in the time of the first workings of the Lord in me". And he "took leave of father and mother, and all other relations, and travelled up and down as a stranger on the earth".

In an earlier age he would have been a Cuthbert or a Guthlac . . .

Until, "being in his usual retirement to God upon a very great hill, called Pendle", a "bare moorland ridge", about eighteen-hundred feet above sea-level, between Nelson and Clitheroe on the borders of Yorkshire and Lancashire, "his mind was moved of the Lord to go up to the top of it, which he did, with difficulty, it was so very steep and high". Where he had, like William

Langland on the Malvern Hills, a Vision of a "fair field full of folk" . . .

He saw "people as thick as motes in the sun, that should in time be brought home to the Lord, that there might be but one shepherd and one sheep-fold in all the earth". And he also saw "that he was to go forth" to begin the "great work of God" . . . and his "eye was directed northward, beholding a great people in white raiment that should receive him and his message in those parts". And then "upon this mountain he was moved of the Lord to sound forth His great and notable day, as if he had been in a great auditory . . . and from thence went north, as the Lord had shown him, so that the Lord was his Leader . . ."

He "travelled swiftly through the Dales" . . . where he "found the Westmoreland Seekers", groups of people scattered over a wide area in a "loose organisation", who were "eagerly awaiting fresh light in their search for Truth".

And, according to the Official Minutes, "these momentous weeks saw the birth of The Society of Friends".

⋆　　⋆　　⋆

"In a day of shams", wrote William James, "it was a religion of veracity rooted in spiritual inwardness, and a return to something more like the original Gospel Truth than men had ever known in England . . . Everyone who confronted George Fox personally, from Oliver Cromwell down to county magistrates and jailers, seems to have acknowledged his spiritual sagacity and capacity, his superior power . . ."

Yet he was "knocked down" on many occasions, "kicked and trampled upon by the people", whipped, dragged out of towns, several times "handed over to the mob, at whose hands he received so severe a beating with switches and staves that he became unconscious" . . . and imprisoned in "foul dungeons" again and again.

And in his own words, "his Friends, in their beginnings, were jeered at, pelted in stocks and pillory with ordure and slop buckets", and "well whipt for professing Quakers", and imprisoned – men and women and even children alike.

Today, three hundred years later, they are a respectable part

188

of the Sunday furniture in the Christian parlour . . . but *then* they were swept under the Christian carpet – and stamped on into the wicked bargain.

However, through their patience and meekness under suffering they were "enabled to make converts by thousands among the common folk" . . . because "Christian qualities matter much more than Christian dogmas".

And Pendle Hill is still there, with a "rough cairn at the top", and breath-taking vistas across the landscape. Westward there's the sea "girdling the Lancashire Coast", and to the north it's much as he saw: the Fell country, "mounting steadily until the view is closed by the rugged Lakeland Hills". Even without the memory of George Fox, it's "an inspiring sight at all times of the year", but, writes Elfrida Vipont Foulds, an historian of the Friends, "when the late snows still glitter on the peaks, few can fail to catch some echoes of that sounding of the Day of the Lord which glorified these moorland solitudes in 1652".

Holy ground, surely?

And even the climb and the fresh air will do you good.

★   ★   ★

Or what about any of the old Meeting Houses established by the Friends?

There he'd be, "declaring the Day of the Lord" at a fair, or by the "Market Cross", and along would come an "abundance of priests and professors" to "dispute" with him.

"This is not a fit place to preach in", they'd say. "Why will you not go into the church?"

With himself calling their buildings "steeple-houses" and worse . . . and he'd "exhort the people to come out from these temples made with hands, and wait to receive the Spirit of the Lord, that they might know themselves to be the temples of God". For, as he said, "that house was not the Church, but the people were the Church, with Christ the Head".

So the early Friends needed no "special place" for worship, "no altar nor furnishings", and would meet in their own houses: though, eventually, as their numbers grew, they did build austere Meeting Houses or adapt barns and other buildings . . . even that Abbot's Kitchen at Glastonbury.

Many of them survive, each beautiful in its own way . . .

Swarthmoor, near Ulverton in Lancashire, was one of the first fruits: a "cottage and barn" with the "paths paved that Friends may go dry to the Meeting . . ."

Or Jordans in Buckinghamshire, "amongst orchards close to a barn said to be made from the timbers of the *Mayflower* in which the Pilgrim Fathers sailed" . . . with William Penn, founder of Pennsylvania, buried in the graveyard. "A simple building with transomed leaded windows", says William Anderson, "its interior sings with peacefulness and silence".

And that "silence" is most of the meaning, because the Friends have no singing, no spoken prayers, and no preaching, and merely sit quietly . . . their meeting together *being* their worship. True, occasionally one of them may be "moved by the Spirit" to "utter" a few words of "ministry" . . . usually some thought or story or verse which he or she believes will "speak to the condition of the Friends present".

Goat Lane in Norwich, Come-to-Good in Cornwall, Lancaster, Colthouse near Hawshead by Esthwaite Water in the Lake District . . .

You'll find simplicity, plain wood, unadorned walls, space, light, a sense of calm, gentle restraint . . . peace . . . that stillness in which you have the "perfect freedom" to hear the "still, small voice . . ."

*   *   *

Or what about any country churchyard?

Not necessarily the most famous . . . though Stoke Poges, north of Slough in Buckinghamshire, would obviously have slightly more sense of place than some others. Because Thomas Gray is said to have written his *Elegy* in the churchyard of St Giles Church, and him buried inside.

Nothing much has changed in two hundred years.

True, that square tower is no longer "ivy-mantled", and there hasn't been a "moping owl" in it since the nearest game-keeper knows when . . . but there are the thirteenth-century flint walls and stone cornerings, the timber porch and nave roof, stained-glass, lectern and altar and pulpit, the "boast of heraldry, the pomp of power . . ."

And there, outside, are the "narrow cells" where the "forefathers of the hamlet sleep", with "uncouth rhymes and shapeless sculpture decked . . ."

Yes, all the well-known words, even hackneyed: we hear them at school . . . and hardly ever have to bother with them again after the exams. But they speak truth about the human condition . . . because ever since kings and queens have worn crowns, ever since warriors have held clubs or swords or guns, Ambition *has* mocked the "useful toil" of the weak, Grandeur *has* smiled disdainfully at the "short and simple annals of the poor". And "chill Penury" *has* "repressed their noble rage", and frozen the "genial current" of their souls.

They built the churches and cathedrals and palaces and Manor houses, and lived in hovels, saw their children die from hunger while my Lord and his Lady feasted, were killed by their Brothers whom their kings called their enemies . . . and none of it any less true because it now happens in slightly less obvious ways. After all, there are votes to be counted, General Elections to be won or lost.

But you don't need to go to Stoke Poges to pay the "passing tribute of a sigh" . . . your own nearest churchyard will do as well for holy ground in which to be "mindful of the unhonoured dead", with *them* honouring the ground and making it holy, not the words of any priest.

And John Donne, though indeed "much possessed by death", also held that your churchyard is the "holy suburb of Heaven", in which "we but wait for the bright morning of Resurrection, the which, when come, will be more than recompense".

*   *   *

With Thomas Traherne drawing the happy conclusion: "Your enjoyment of the world is never right", says he, "till every morning you awake in Heaven, see yourself in your Father's Palace, and look upon the skies, the earth, and the air as Celestial Joys, having such a reverend esteem of all as if you were among the Angels".

For *this* is Heaven . . . nor need we be out of it.

Two Windows and a Statue

"My subject is War", wrote Wilfred Owen, "and the pity of War".

And the "pity of War" may be felt in most cathedrals: all you have to do is visit the Chapel of Remembrance . . . but it may be felt more poignantly than in many if you go to Worcester.

North Porch, left turn, walk up past the Transept – and there, just to the rear of the Pulpit, is St George's Chapel, dedicated to the Glorious Dead of the County Regiment and All Other Branches of the Armed Forces of the Crown . . . the Fallen of Both World Wars who Gave their Todays for our Tomorrows, who Died that we might Live . . .

Yes, "the bugles calling for them from sad shires".

Nothing more remarkable about the place than any one of the others: stained-glass, the Flags and Battle Honours of the Regiment, a Book of Remembrance . . . beautiful lettering and illumination . . .

Read a few of the names: Officers and Gentlemen, Sergeants, Corporals, Privates, the Long and the Short and the Tall . . . and spare them two minutes of your silence.

"They shall grow not old, as we that are left grow old . . ."

True, names are little to go by: we don't know what sort of men they were, how they lived, why they fought, the way they died . . . all we know is that they're dead, and that women mourned them as women have always mourned in time of war.

And then, perhaps, remember all the other Chapels of Remembrance, all the other names you'll never read, all the men, the women, the children who never knew a father: American, British, French, German, Italian, Japanese, Polish, Russian . . . all the tribes of the earth, out of every kindred, and tongue, and people, and nation.

"Age shall not weary them, nor the years condemn".

What's two minutes in a lifetime?

*   *   *

And then walk back the way you've come, past the Pulpit and

the Transept, all those columns, on past the Porch . . . and there, on your left, is the Edward Elgar Memorial Window: great venue for music, Worcester . . . you know, one of the famous homes of the Three Choirs Festival with Hereford and Gloucester.

Again, nothing more remarkable about the window than any one of a hundred others: a portrait, an inscription, the dates.

But Edward Elgar wrote the various *Pomp and Circumstance* marches, *Crown Imperial, Land of Hope and Glory* . . . trumpets and drums, the tunes of war . . . songs of battle . . .

Not that the Dead marched to *that* music: much more likely to have been *Pack Up Your Troubles in Your Old Kit-Bag* or *The Girl I Left Behind Me* . . . *Lili Marlene* . . .

But Edward Elgar's was the Official Music as performed at Ceremonial Parades and Victory Marches and other celebrations – those times when Medals Will Be Worn and Salutes Given and Taken . . .

And there he is now, his face idealised: strong, noble . . . haunted . . .

For he also wrote the *Cello Concerto,* the last of his full-scale orchestral works.

As the First World War had dragged on in mud and senseless slaughter he "increasingly felt despair and disillusionment", and he seemed to die with the dying. Then he was persuaded to move to Sussex, and "heard wonderful new music, real wood sounds, and other laments which should be in a War Symphony".

And these "laments" begin the *Cello Concerto* . . .

Nineteen-eighteen, the Armistice, the end of the First World War . . .

"Everything good and nice and clean and fresh and sweet is far away", he wrote, "never to return".

No more marches, silent the trumpets, muffled the drums . . . merely those faint bugles sounding the *Last Post* across the "sad shires".

Because in his final music we hear his *Anthem for Doomed Youth,* the expression of a grief that is too deep for tears, the anguish of a man who suffered with the suffering, died with the dying, and was buried with the Dead. It wasn't about "deeds, or lands, nor anything about glory, honour, might, majesty, dominion, or power" ... but about the battle-fields after the battles, mud, bodies, flies, futility ...

For him, if you can hear that music, every dawn must have broken open "like a wound that bleeds afresh". Because "men have bled where no wounds were" ... and he bled.

Peace, Edward Elgar, Love and Joy and Peace.

*　　*　　*

It should be perfectly obvious by now that I'm uneasy in cathedrals, and that when the light fails on a winter's afternoon I'd rather stroll through certain half-deserted streets than attend a performance of Choral Evensong. There's something about the weight of all that dead grey stone, the memories of those who built ... the history of the Church ...

But, for the sake of a dead girl, I still occasionally go into Norwich Cathedral. True, I walk in the long way round to avoid a Memorial Window to a County Regiment: First World War, the trenches, men about to go over the top with fixed-bayonets ... all in tasteful stained-glass.

It's those fixed-bayonets I'm avoiding ...

"I am the enemy you killed, my friend.
I knew you in this dark: for so you frowned
Yesterday through me as you jabbed and killed.
I parried – but my hands were loath and cold.

195

Let us sleep now . . ."
No, I don't need any reminding about the "pity of War".

*　　*　　*

But this dead girl: Seems that she was the secretary of the then bishop, who was extremely fond of her, and terribly distressed at her tragically early death. There were even sly whispers that, er, he might have been, er, you know, at bit *too* fond. Anyway, when she died, he himself laid her to rest, and had this statue erected to her memory.

"Near the High Altar", said somebody, "so that he could see her every time he officiated. But it was moved when he died".

"Embarrassing to the powers that be", said somebody else.

And that was that: the beginnings of the story of Sweet Vi.

*　　*　　*

So, the first chance I got, I went to have a look for myself . . . and it was very much as I'd been told.

She's tucked away in the far corner of the North Transept, so close to the wall that it's almost impossible to read the inscription on what is now the back of the plinth. Yes, bit of a mystery there – as what's an inscription doing where it can hardly be seen? The result of a discreet shifting into decent obscurity by those powers-that-be?

Life-size statue, ivory-white marble, beautiful girl, serene, her very presence such a sweetness breathes that all the other effigies in there are made to look what they are: things of bronze and stone, lifeless, beyond the reach of sympathy. She's kneeling where prayer has been valid, hands touching gently, arms resting against the buds of her little breasts, her head raised to visions of stained-glass glories across the Transept, sudden in a shaft of sunlight.

Violet, the only child of Penry and Evelyn Morgan, lovely and beloved, who, towards the end of February, 1919, at the age of twenty years, passed from this life to whatever awaits us all. And was laid to rest in Caistor churchyard by Bertram, bishop of Norwich.

"Sweet Vi", says the inscription . . . and she's by her Bishop's

196

Door, so that if ever he came in again she'd be the first to see him.

"Many visitors imagine that this white kneeling figure is one of the New Testament saints", says the Official Guide, "and there are others who question its propriety . . . and it was moved to its present relatively inconspicuous place by order of the Dean and Chapter some years ago, who did not feel entirely at ease about its form or the very romantic and flowery words in the inscription".

★　　★　　★

I started asking around, checking hints and guesses, reading books and yellowed press-cuttings . . .

Bertram Pollock. Headmaster of Wellington College for seventeen years. Aloof, impatient, not given to revealing either his thoughts or his emotions. Formal, deferential, politic, cautious, and meticulous, Bishop here from 1910 to 1942. Main interest the opposition to the Revision of the Book of Common Prayer.

Had this austere man called her his "Sweet Vi"? and then made these private words a public gesture?

True, he did make an autumnal marriage with another secretary years afterwards, and so knew that leaping delight where the fire and the rose are one.

Variations began to appear: It wasn't him but the parents who paid for the statue – which wasn't anywhere near the High Altar.

People disagreed: "It *was* the bishop . . . and he had a replica made which he kept on the landing of the stairs in the Bishop's Palace, so he could see her every time he went up to bed".

"Are you *sure* it wasn't the parents who paid for it? Only *they* were supposed to have had a replica, which they kept in an alcove with a sliding curtain and special lighting".

"No, it was the bishop. He was devoted to her, and there was a lot of controversy. Those times were narrow. Tongues wagged".

Some liked the statue, some didn't: "Bit sentimental. Visitors mistake it for the Virgin Mary. One lady actually looped a rosary around the hands. Don't want *that* in a Church of England cathedral, now *do* you?"

And from many raised eyebrows and knowing shrugs it was

obvious that, even after sixty years, the faint suggestions of scandal were dying hard. Talk about a storm in a Transept!

★　　★　　★

Then I read what his wife wrote about him: "His first years at Norwich were lonely ones", for he was a "bachelor in an exalted position". And she went on to describe him romping at the seaside with their only child, a girl . . . paddling . . .

And the more I discovered, the more I responded to this man who had measured out his life with formulated phrases. I don't care what wagging tongues have clacked, what slanderers have whispered . . . because my Brother in Christ must have been human all the way up. Shy, yes, and even perhaps awkward. But he had heard the mermaids singing, seen the sunlight weaving in the hair of a girl . . . and his love now warms those cold grey stones for me.

★　　★　　★

One last little creative flourish.

Several people have now told me that when the statue was going to be moved it was destined for the Cloisters, as far away from the inside of the cathedral as possible. But, says the growing legend, a couple arrived and demanded to see the Dean, said they'd attended a Seance in London a few evenings before . . . where a girl's voice kept breaking in:

"Norwich", it whispered, "the cathedral . . . don't put me out in the cold, please don't put me out . . . don't put me out in the cold . . . please . . . the cold, not out in the cold . . ."

So she was moved to where she now kneels and waits . . .

Sleep, Little Sister, you were loved in your life, and remembered after your death . . . and who needs any greater warmth?

★　　★　　★

And Salisbury Cathedral is another exception: yes, that lovely Constable view across the water-meadows beside the River Avon is still possible, that majestically soaring spire and length of roof, all those delicate pinnacles and traceried windows, the high clouds behind, and the trees a frame.

Mind you, the stone is never that pale Romantic Gothic, not *these* industrial days . . . and it's crumbling badly, lots of restoration being done behind the scaffolding.

And there are all the usual pomps and circumstances inside: Cloisters, Chapter House, War Memorial Chapel, clustered columns of polished Purbeck marble, the tombs of bishops and earls and knights . . . though Richard Jefferies is also remembered, which is a bonus for all who love the English landscape and have an ear for its music.

But please walk on down towards the Lady Chapel at the very far end behind the High Altar, for there is one of the most profound and searching works of Religious Art of this or any other century.

*　*　*

The light is passionately blue as you approach, even purple, especially in the morning with the sun slanting in from the east, with geometrical scatterings of crimson, rays of pale sapphire, squared jewels of emerald green and sombre yellow . . . descending gold . . .

Five lancets of this intense light, side by side, darkness between, tall, the one in the middle taller than the other two pairs, framed in those narrow arches of stone.

At first it looks an abstraction, patches of brilliant colour ribbed in rectangles, crossed and wandering with lines and upward swirlings, beautiful . . . but . . . well, hasn't it all been done before by John Piper in Coventry Cathedral? Already a bit dated? A passing fashion?

And then you begin to see the faces, the figures, Christ . . . yes, the Crucified in that central lancet, high and hanging, tortured . . . then the other faces, other figures, bars of iron, chalices, a cockerel crowing, barbed-wire, solitude . . . darkness at noon . . .

"Who are these? Wherefore rock they, purgatorial shadows?"

*　*　*

199

These are the *Prisoners of Conscience,* a heart-wrenching glory by Gabriel Loire. And, in the words of the Dean, they "speak to the heart of those who are prepared to stand and look, and read what is written in the glass, and hear what the window is saying".

Gabriel Loire is a French artist and craftsman with a studio-workshop on the outskirts of Chartres, and he has lived all his life in "close familiarity" with the wonders of the stained-glass in that magnificent cathedral. "Those windows", wrote Henry Adams, "claim to be the most splendid colour decorations the world ever saw, since no other material, neither silk, nor gold, and no opaque colour lain on with a brush, can compare with translucent glass . . ."

Well, yes, the windows of Chartres are indeed "most splendid colour decorations", and there are certainly more of them – and these five lancets are at least as beautiful . . . but they are more than merely "splendid" . . . *they are "about" what should be one of the deep shames of our times.*

Chartres has glass the colour of blood: *these* are drawn in living blood, shed by the men and women who have "challenged the easy assumption that might confers right, who have stood firm for truth against the lie . . . who have upheld the dignity of the human person against falsehood and tyranny".

And the Dean quotes some words of Alexander Solzhenitsyn to illuminate the theme: "Violence does not exist alone and cannot survive in isolation. It is inevitably bound up with the lie".

★   ★   ★

The truth, then, the truth of *our* violence.

Christ the Prisoner, the Interrogated, the Tortured, the Mocked, the Crucified . . . and *we* the Crucifiers: for we continue to nail the Son of God on all manner of our contemporary crosses. So *His* Passion and Death fills that central trinity of pain: the Trial of the Innocent before the State, the Crowning of this King by the mercenaries of Caesar, the Crucifixion . . . that Sacred Head Sore Wounded . . .

"See, see, where Christ's blood streams in the firmament!"

And He's excruciated with His Brothers and Sisters in the

flanking lancets, their sorrows *His* sorrows, their agony *His* agony, their screaming *His* cry of deriliction – their sufferings the "suffering of God in the life of the world".

Amnesty International will give you all the facts: Russians torture Russians, the South African Security Police use their whips on the flesh of Africans, the Turks and the Chileans and the Iranians clip the electrodes to the genitals of Turks and Chileans and Iranians . . .

And as for the Americans in Viet Nam!

How terrible! how monstrous!

Yes, "night comes blood-black . . ."

And how easy to say when it's the *others* doing it.

But have there *never* been Prisoners of Conscience in *this* country? Or do *we* define the "crime" to exclude conscience?

Has Innocence *never* been dragged before the State? Have the police *never* lied? never clubbed or kicked *any* prisoner?

Have suspects *never* been tortured in Northern Ireland? or don't you believe the Reports of your own Commissions of Inquiry?

When do gunmen become soldiers? are freedom-fighters ever terrorists?

Have *all* our recent wars been just ones?

Or isn't *that* what *you* mean by the truth of violence?

"What the window will say", writes the Dean, "will depend on what each is able to receive. Each of us will know ourselves being searched in the deep centres of our being".

How deep are *you* willing to be searched?

Or is that cockerel crowing for the third time?

Resurrection, Cookham

"With its green surrounded by pretty houses and pleasant high street", it says here, "Cookham draws many visitors. The river here also has great charm, enhanced by the hanging woods of Cliveden. In the village stands an old sarsen stone . . ."

Well, yes, all very delightful, a lovely place, much like hundreds of highly-coloured picture-postcards on sale in a thousand gift-shops and newsagents . . . but, er . . .

But Stanley Spencer was born in Cookham, lived here forty-nine of his sixty-eight years, and died here . . . and to him it was the New Jerusalem we've heard so much about already, an Earthly Paradise on the River Thames: for he saw the Divine "as clearly in a puddle or a dustbin as others in mountain scenery or a Gothic vault".

Indeed, for *him* "those feet *did* walk in England's green and pleasant land" . . . the boots of Christ trudged up the High Street most mornings.

And *this* ground is holy.

*　　*　　*

Any of the biographies and coffee-table Art Books will give you many of the facts: born in 1891, six brothers and two sisters, father an organist and teacher of music, good mother . . .

"I with all my life I could have remained tied to her apron strings. It would have suited me, mostly in the kitchen . . . long talks and plenty of cups of tea".

So an unfashionable happy childhood, a "Heavenly experience", took to drawing at an early age . . . all the usual and useful words.

What matters is what he painted and what manner of man he was.

"Sometimes", he said, "I get a plain glimpse of that Earthly Paradise" . . . and he obviously enjoyed "prolonged exultation over things that to others are entirely commonplace". When he was "going about the village" he was "aware of a wonderful something which was everywhere to be felt" all around him,

"Heaven as clear as the Cookham day". He could "see more in litter and rubbish and a village dustbin than in a cathedral", because these things "were so human, so closely bound up with people's lives". And in this "beautiful Wholeness" he saw holiness . . . and, even though he was never a Christian in any dreary Credal way, he began to understand that Christianity wasn't merely a "thing of the past but an experience of the present".

And his "present" was always Cookham and his friends who lived there, and he seemed to have a "loving knowledge" of every stone and tile and window, all the bricks, pavements, railings, flowers, grass, faces.

"Cookham seems to me possessed by a sacred presence . . ."

So when he painted *The Visitation* of the Virgin Mary to Elizabeth, mother of John the Baptist, the two women are Dot and Emmie, young daughters of the local butcher, both a bit shy, and wearing their best Sunday frocks newly ironed . . . with the pub and the houses of Cookham to be seen through the open door.

The Last Supper takes a place in a malt-house near his home, and when he painted *Christ Carrying the Cross* it's in the High Street, his Gran lived in the ivy-covered cottage, and various friends and neighbours are standing around watching . . . with two local building-labourers lugging their ladders in the rear of the procession – only glad to see somebody else "doing a bit of carrying" for a change.

True, the place is transformed, even transfigured, there's no horror, only wonder that the "King of the World passes on His way to death", and all the people looking out of the open windows have their curtains billowing out like the wings of choiring Angels – but this Via Dolorosa remains Cookham High Street.

Dozens of paintings, then, hundreds of formal drawings and casual sketches, *The Annunciation, Marriage at Cana, Christ in the Wilderness, Christ Preaching at the Regatta, The Last Supper, The Betrayal, The Crucifixion* . . . none of them far from the house where he was born, with him always as close to Heaven as when he was a boy.

And everything coming together in *Resurrection, Cookham.*

★ ★ ★

He'd always "found graveyards homely places, full of human touches", with "village people apt to be absorbed by burials, wreaths, and the like" . . . but *this* painting began when he read the Sermons of John Donne, and painted him *Arriving in Heaven* . . . with Heaven being Widbrook Common behind the High Street.

Well, as we've seen, John Donne has that phrase about the churchyard being the "Holy suburb of Heaven" – and this hooked Stanley's imagination . . . because there was only one possible churchyard so far as he was concerned: "Cookham's would surely be the scene of our final resurrection, the Thames radiant and serene like the Heavenly Jordan . . ." He even knew the time of day when the light would be best for painting: "At a quarter-to-three on the afternoon of a Tuesday in May".

No, not quite the trumpet-crack of dawn, but, as he explained: "No one is in any hurry. Here and there things slowly move off, but in the main they resurrect to such a state of joy that they are content to stay *where* they have resurrected. In this life we experience a kind of resurrection when we arrive at a state of awareness, a state of being in love . . ."

It's a large painting, eighteen feet long by nine feet high, which now hangs in the Tate Gallery, London . . . only about twenty-five miles down the river from Cookham.

The scene is the churchyard, viewed from near the gate of the vicarage, with the church in the background, and the "Thames radiant and serene" in the top left-hand distance. In the middle of the church is the porch with roses, roses, roses round the door, there are open tombs and graves, headstones and crosses and memorials . . . and the dead resurrecting all over the place, sliding back their granite slabs, pushing up through the earth, reading their own epitaphs, some yawning and stretching after their long sleep, some reclining at their ease, or kneeling or sitting or standing, some clothed in best Sunday suits, some in flowing white robes, some naked and enjoying the sunshine on their new flesh, mostly English, though some are Negroes, some looking out of their vaults as though hardly able to believe it, two old friends talking as though they'd never stopped, the Good "rising serenely from the grass", the not so Good "looking out despairingly from the jaws of turf from which they struggle to free themselves".

No everlasting Hell for Stanley, then, no eternal punishments: the "wicked" are having a bit of trouble, that's all, as not even this Second Birth is any easier than the first . . . but they'll make it, eventually. This, of course, is an ancient Christian heresy, the idea of ultimate reconciliation of all and everyone to God, with none damned . . .

Yes, "All shall be well, and all shall be well, and all manner of thing shall be well".

For which Christians have damned and burnt one another alive.

But there are no heretics in *this* Paradise, only men and women who haven't always lived up to the best they knew . . . and who there even *thinks* of picking up the first stone?

"I cannot see Christ standing in Hell and giving a turn to some thumbscrew", said Stanley, "or scorching someone's shinbone, and being quite happy about it".

And so Christ sits in the shade of the cool porch, with children in His arms, and God is leaning over the back of the small throne in a friendly sort of pleased way, fingering His Son's hair. If there's no Hell, there's certainly no Judgement . . . so they're merely watching, enjoying all the obvious happiness.

Saints and Prophets are ranged on larger thrones along the wall of the church, even Moses with the Tables of the Law, all posing as if they're in the Sistine Chapel on one of those interminable Sundays After Trinity, but nobody seems to be taking much notice of them.

Stanley is there "in the company of his friends and forebears", naked, "stilled by the wonder of it" . . . and his wife appears several times: "Hilda mooches along and slowly climbs over the stile. She wears a favourite dress of hers". And "by the ivy-covered tower" she's the woman "brushing the earth and grass off her husband, much as Ma brushed Pa down when he went to London".

"If we're going to meet God", she's saying, "I'll have you tidy".

Again, "you see Hilda smelling a flower. She wonders about its scent and pushes it against her face". She wears a jumper he liked, "one that had been pulled into being very flopped from much washing . . ." And some of the other women wear more of her dresses . . . for he loved her, and wrote long passionate letters to her even after she had died.

Yes, earthly and sexual love were the gates of Heavenly Love, with the Song of Songs the Gospel of *this* Kingdom . . . for her "belly is like an heap of wheat set about with lilies", her breasts "like to clusters of grapes".

And there, in that top-left hand distance, on the Thames are the pleasure-steamers ferrying people across into Heaven . . .

Yes, Stanley Spencer . . . Yes, in gentle thunder!

Heaven *can* be experienced on earth, Paradise is *now* . . . all we have to do is resurrect into Love new every morning.

★ ★ ★

Mind you, he didn't manage to paint the half of it – for how could he possibly squeeze in what was happening all over the other Cookhams of this world on that Glad Day?

You'd need more than a few dozen Sistine Chapels!

So stroll through the churchyard, on down the path towards the stile and the banks of the Thames . . . and there's Julian of Norwich with Guthlac of Croyland, hand-in-hand, both of them munching on a shared Worcester apple, taking turns to bite . . .

"I knew all manner of thing would be well", she says, "I just *knew*!"

Thomas Cromwell and Henry Tudor, stripped to the waist, are hard at work repairing a yard or two of the crumbling wall at the back of the church, with George Fox mixing the mortar . . .

"Neglected", says Henry. "Should have been seen to years ago".

Elizabeth and Mary are cutting the bread for cucumber sandwiches, the picnic tea being in ten minutes . . .

"That's if Hugh Lattimer can get any cucumbers", says Mary. "There was quite a queue at the counter".

"One of the worst puns I've *ever* heard", says William of Malmesbury. "Reminds me of the one about Angles and Angels".

"Have you seen Bede yet?" says Aidan of Lindisfarne.

"Public Library", says William. "Started to revise his *History* in the light of the latest developments".

And there's Thomas à Becket arguing with Thomas Stearns

Eliot about *Murder in the Cathedral:* "You wrote better than you knew", he says, "and beyond your understanding . . . but you got *some* of it very wrong, believe you me".

"Saint and Martyr rule from the tomb", says the other Thomas. "But I *do* wish you'd call me Tom".

And there are John Clare and Richard Jefferies, kneeling by the hedge, teaching Patrick and Columba the English names of the wildflowers . . . and the other Clare is at last embracing her beloved Francis, with him having woven columbines and campions into all her lovely hair, and oak-tufts and honeysuckle in small buds, bluebells, forget-me-nots and wood-ruff, hyacinth and creeping-jenny . . .

And David Herbert Lawrence is smiling, and listening to Hugh of Lincoln telling him about how John Ruskin was doing exactly the same sort of thing with a beautiful young girl along the lane – except that he was using roses from the church porch . . .

And Dante, still vaguely astonished that this isn't Florence with all the flowers there are around, is explaining to Beatrice and Dorothy Sayers what he *really* meant by those "faces of living flame and wings of gold descending into the white rose . . ."

And William Blake and Isaac Newton are playing marbles against John Donne and Wilfed Owen, with Jane Austen bringing them icecream in cones – though she's having a chocolate-covered chopped-nut vanilla herself . . .

"Wait for us!" calls John of the Cross. "Only Teresa had a stone in her shoe!"

And there, over the stile, in the shallows of the river, kneeling, Jerome is having his back scrubbed by Etheldreda of Ely, both of them naked, laughing and splashing like children.

"After you with the brush and soap!" yells Hilda of Whitby. "Thomas Traherne has promised to do mine!"

Caedmon and Chaucer, while waiting for the next pleasure-steamer across, are feeding the fish with pieces of bread . . . the entire Bach family and Louis Armstrong and Bessie Smith and Edward Elgar are all improvising a lullaby for Perotine Massey's morning-new baby . . . Cuthbert and Richeldis are building a little wooden nest-box for the pair of Goldeneye they've discovered upstream. . . .

"There are only two recorded cases of them breeding here",

says Himself, "so it would be quite a scoop if we could pull it off!"

Gerald Manley Hopkins and Winefride have started their picnic already, sharing with five Franscican nuns: you can tell they've been Franscicans because their familiar habits of perfection are spread out all over the grass to sit on, and they've rolled up their shifts for cushions . . .

And here come . . .

*   *   *

But why not people your own Heaven?

Stanley Spencer did.

Cookham, on the Sweet Thames in Berkshire, *that's* the place – though anywhere else will do, anywhere else in the world.

Make your own ground holy.

Because if *we* can imagine such tender glories – well, what will the *real* place be like?

Queen of More than Ireland

Well, we began with St Patrick wandering the Holy Land of Ireland all those years of the long ago, so where better to be ending?

With miracles galore still abounding . . . as why wouldn't they be?

*   *   *

Consider Knock, a wee village on a gentle rise of pasture just to the north of Claremorris in the Plains of County Mayo, with the name of it meaning "the hill" in the Gaelic . . . and Croagh Patrick itself not more than twenty-five Irish miles to the west.

Well now, a hundred years ago of the not so long ago, give or take ten years to be sparing, on a wet Thursday night in August – and isn't it always raining? But, for two hours or three of that night, with the fifteen sworn witnesses, the Blessed Virgin Mary was "observed motionless, raised slightly above ground level, Her back to the southern wall of the Parish church". With Her, one on the left and the other on the right, She had St Joseph, Her Most Sacred Spouse, and St John the Evangelist. Near them was "an Altar, on it a Lamb and a Cross". And the two hours or three they hovered there, with never a word out of them.

One of the witnesses, Bridget Trench, with seventy-five years of such weather behind her, was insistent on a strange lack of rain around the Vision: "I went immediately to kiss the feet of the Virgin", she said, "but felt nothing in the embrace but the wall, and wondered why I could not feel with my hands the figures which I had so plainly and distinctly seen. It was raining very heavily at the time", she said, "but no rain fell where the figures were. I felt the ground carefully with my hands, and it was perfectly dry".

True, there *were* the stories circulating that it was "all done with a magic-lantern", and, sad to tell, the young Assistant Priest was caught trying to duplicate the Vision on the end wall of his next church a few years later . . . which is *not* to say that he

211

worked it at Knock. For aren't the young always given to over-enthusiasm? Wasn't it bad enough for him that he was ever caught at all? And wouldn't he carry the penance of it to his mortal grave?

Anyway, imagine the commotion of the Faithful, the running to and fro, the hither and thithering . . .

The first cure was reported ten days later, when a twelve-year-old deaf girl heard the voice of her mother for the first time in her silent life, Glory be! And there were a hundred more miracles by the Spring of the next year, with lame men leaping, women healed of the womanly troubles, and the pilgrims beginning to hack bits of cement off that gable wall . . . for all you had to do was "dissolve it in Holy Water", sip a wee mouthful, and you had the defeating of disease and affliction.

When the cement was diluted over a grateful country, and it gone from the gable end, they took the mortar, with the stones falling and leaving holes . . . so the wall had to be repaired and boarded against them, or they'd have had the church down, surely. And, as a further precaution, the Parish priest had a notice made, advising pilgrims that "the clay below the wall was just as efficacious as the wall itself". And then, says Don McPhee, working for *The Guardian*, your man "watched as an extensive area of ground was eroded and the long-suffering miraculous wall all but undermined".

Well, that was over a century and an Official Papal Visit ago, and there's the grand concrete Basilica of Our Lady Queen of Ireland at the place now, half-a-million pilgrims a year, "with", says Don McPhee, "a fast train to Claremorris from Dublin, a waiting bus direct to the shrine, Holy Water on tap, eighteen Confessional boxes, a dozen or so Masses a day, and flush lavatories".

And (as who could doubt?) the inevitable gift-shops, where you can buy Holy pictures of the Blessed Virgin Mary, sweets, Holy statues of Herself, cigarettes, Holy medals, sticks of Knock rock, and plastic bottles in the shape of the Holy Virgin for to be carrying away your Holy Water.

*   *   *

And so it goes, with statues of Herself smiling all over Ireland, the Mother of Mercy inclining Her Holy Head towards Her "poor banished children of Eve", turning Her Holy Eyes in their direction, weeping . . . beckoning them with Her Holy Hands . . .

Literally.

Because in Ireland, not to mention elsewhere, Her statues smile, move their heads, weep tears, extend their hands, sway from side to side, and occasionally levitate.

★   ★   ★

Again, consider Ballinspittle, another wee village, this time eighteen miles or twenty south-west of the fine City of Cork, with the name of it meaning "the mouth of the ford of the hospital" in the Gaelic . . . and the place merely the latest square yard of holy ground.

Well then, one very recent year ago, a week or two before the Feast of the Assumption, which celebrates the Bodily Assumption of Our Blessed Lady into the Courts of Heaven, being the fifteenth of August, two elderly women took an evening stroll out of the village, and up the lane to the Grotto . . . as why wouldn't they, being devout Roman Catholics with never a word said against them. And in the Grotto, as in many another all over Ireland and elsewhere, there's this blue and white

213

painted statue of Herself, with a halo of twelve electric-light bulbs, doing duty as the Stars of Her Crown.

And, as they stood praying in the twilight, the statue moved, "swaying back and forth" . . . and the "harder they looked, the more obvious was the movement".

True, there *are* the swift explanations: that "people standing still tend to sway, and what they are looking at appears to move". In the light of day "this movement can be discerned against other objects, but in darkness this cannot be done". And this "sensation of movement is also exaggerated by the glare of light" around the statue's head.

With some of these explanations more complicated: that the "human-eye responds much more rapidly to bright lights than dim objects", a "bright light being seen where it actually is" – while a "dim object will be seen where it was a fraction of a second ago", this interval known as "latency" or the "interval of perception". So that "head or eye movements produce a corresponding movement of the image on the retina . . . indistinguishable from the supposed movements of the object".

Not that Ballinspittle would hear a word of such talk.

*   *   *

The next night there were forty people at the Grotto, and "most agreed" the statue was moving. By the end of the week a thousand a night were processing up that lane, a field was converted into a car-park, and there was a steady trade in hot-dogs and fish-and-chips from mobile vans.

On the Feast of the Assumption twenty thousand pilgrims assembled, many taking advantage of the new daily coach service from Dublin, lots with cameras or binoculars, some with home-movie equipment to record the miracle . . . and the statue has been seen to "sway to and fro, or from side to side, with hands parting or head rocking".

The Roman Catholic Church is "preaching prudence and caution", and maintaining that "all natural explanations will have to be examined over a lengthy period before a conclusion can be reached".

But in the meantime, according to Paul Johnson of *The Guardian*, "the shops are doing a roaring trade, the local public house has never been busier".

And now the reports are beginning to come in from County Kerry, Ballydesmond, Waterford, and Court Macsherry... other statues moving... even talking...

"Glory be!" my beloved old Irish Gran used to say, "but aren't we the religious people!"

★   ★   ★

And yet, and yet... there's a sense in which even all this is a sign of our times.

Because it doesn't really matter whether or not these are miracles or delusions, genuine mysteries or the exploitation of the credulous.

What's significant is that so many people believe them to be true, that there's an obvious need for such wonders... even a hunger for concerns of the Spirit...

"The hungry sheep look up, and are not fed..."

For the world is peopled with men and women – and yet it's a man's world, society is patriarchal... and our Christian God is the "Father" in Heaven.

Is there no longer any proper place for the Mother? for that ancient cycle of spontaneous loving and natural birth? happy living and the peaceful acceptance of death as the beginning of resurrection and rebirth into another cycle?

Not only Mary the Virgin, for She is merely the gentle and necessary beginning, but Herself of the Thousand Names, Mother and Mate and Lady of the Wild Things, walking the woods, bathing naked and not ashamed in the lakes and running rivers, as fruitful as the earth itself, as mysterious and magnificent as the Moon.

"The longer Her hour is postponed", wrote Robert Graves, "and therefore the more exhausted by man's irreligious improvidence the natural resources of the soil and sea become, the less merciful will She be".

Which is not to agree with the Radical Feminists, not to demand for the replacement of the patriarchy by a matriarchy – because women at their worst are as bad as men.

But men *and* women, equal and gloriously different, each doing what each does best.

Because to go beyond where the Waste Land ends is to find true holy ground, to join Her "long-omitted feast" . . . and be male *and* female on the Sixth Day in another Eden.

Index

221